The Failures of Socialism in Economic Development

Copyright Page

TITLE: The Failures of Socialism in Economic Development

1ST Edition

Copyright @ 2023

ISBN: 9798223827047

Table of Contents

The Failures of Socialism in Economic Development

By Roberto Miguel Rodriguez

Book Outline

Introduction:

- Defining socialism and its historical context

- Setting the stage for understanding the failure of socialism in economic development

- Exploring the objectives and structure of the book

The Failure of Socialism

- Examining the fundamental flaws in socialist economic systems

- Analyzing the reasons behind the collapse of socialist states

- Comparing the outcomes of socialist and capitalist economies

- Addressing common misconceptions and arguments in defense of socialism

The Economic Stagnation Caused by Socialism

- Investigating the impact of socialist policies on economic growth

- Highlighting examples of countries that experienced economic stagnation under socialist regimes

- Demonstrating the negative consequences of centralized planning and state control

The Erosion of Individual Liberties under Socialist Regimes

- Examining the suppression of civil liberties and human rights in socialist states

- Exploring the limitations on freedom of speech, expression, and assembly

- Discussing the lack of political and personal freedoms under socialist governments

The Inefficiency and Lack of Innovation in Socialist Economies

- Analyzing the economic inefficiencies resulting from socialist policies

- Investigating the lack of innovation and technological progress in centrally planned economies

- Comparing the productivity and efficiency of socialist and capitalist economies

The Unequal Distribution of Wealth and Resources in Socialist Societies

- Discussing the concentration of power and wealth in the hands of the few in socialist systems

- Examining the lack of economic opportunities and social mobility

- Addressing the implications of wealth inequality on societal well-being

The Suppression of Free Speech and Dissent in Socialist States

- Analyzing the censorship and control of information in socialist societies

- Investigating the persecution of political dissidents and activists

- Discussing the implications of limited freedom of expression on societal progress

The Dependency Culture Fostered by Socialist Policies

- Exploring the consequences of welfare state policies and entitlement programs

- Discussing the impact of government dependency on individual motivation and innovation

- Analyzing the long-term implications of a dependency culture on economic development

The Inability of Socialist Governments to Provide Adequate Healthcare and Education

- Investigating the shortcomings of socialist healthcare and education systems

- Analyzing the lack of access, quality, and innovation in these sectors

- Comparing the outcomes of socialist and market-driven approaches to healthcare and education

The Corruption and Lack of Accountability in Socialist Systems

- Examining the prevalence of corruption and nepotism in socialist regimes

- Analyzing the lack of transparency and accountability in government institutions

- Discussing the impact of corruption on economic development and societal well-being

The Environmental Degradation Resulting from Socialist Industrial Policies

- Investigating the environmental consequences of socialist industrialization

- Analyzing the lack of environmental regulations and incentives for sustainability

- Addressing the importance of market-based solutions in promoting environmental conservation

The Failure of Socialist States to Provide Basic Necessities and Improve Living Standards

- Examining the inability of socialist governments to meet the basic needs of their citizens

- Analyzing the persistent poverty and low living standards in socialist societies

- Discussing the role of economic freedom and market-based approaches in improving living conditions

Conclusion:

- Summarizing the key findings and arguments presented in the book

- Reflecting on the lessons learned from the failure of socialism in economic development

- Encouraging educators to engage in critical discussions with their students about the topic

Chapter 1: The Failure of Socialism

The economic stagnation caused by socialism

Introduction:

In this subchapter, we will delve into the economic stagnation caused by socialism, a topic that has been widely debated in the field of economics. By exploring the failures of socialist economies and analyzing the reasons behind their lack of progress, we aim to provide educators with a comprehensive understanding of the detrimental effects of socialism on economic development.

The decline of productivity and innovation:

One of the key factors contributing to economic stagnation under socialism is the lack of incentives for productivity and innovation. Socialist economies, characterized by state control and central planning, often stifle individual creativity and entrepreneurship. In such systems, the absence of competition and market mechanisms leads to complacency and a lack of motivation to excel.

The unequal distribution of wealth and resources:

Another consequence of socialism is the unequal distribution of wealth and resources. Despite the promise of equality, socialist regimes often concentrate power and wealth in the hands of a few elites, while the majority of the population struggles to access basic necessities. This concentration of resources hampers economic growth and perpetuates social and economic disparities.

The erosion of individual liberties:

Socialist regimes often suppress individual liberties, including freedom of speech and dissent. This repression stifles intellectual and creative potential, hindering economic progress. Without the ability to freely exchange ideas and challenge the status quo, innovation and economic development become stagnant.

The dependency culture fostered by socialist policies:

Socialist policies often create a culture of dependency, as citizens come to rely heavily on the state for basic necessities. This dependency hampers individual initiative and self-reliance, discouraging entrepreneurship and hindering economic growth.

The inefficiency and lack of accountability in socialist systems:

Central planning and state control in socialist economies often lead to inefficiency and a lack of accountability. Without the incentives of the market and the mechanisms of competition, there is little pressure for efficient resource allocation or the delivery of quality goods and services.

Conclusion:

The economic stagnation caused by socialism is a result of various factors, including the decline of productivity and innovation, unequal distribution of wealth and resources, erosion of individual liberties, dependency culture, inefficiency, and lack of accountability. It is crucial for educators to understand these failures in order to provide a comprehensive perspective on the limitations and drawbacks of socialist economic systems. By learning from history, we can encourage informed discussions and foster critical thinking among students, ultimately contributing to a more prosperous and equitable society.

The erosion of individual liberties under socialist regimes

In recent years, there has been a growing concern about the erosion of individual liberties under socialist regimes. While proponents of socialism argue that it is a system that promotes equality and social justice, the reality is far from this ideal. Socialist governments often exert control over every aspect of their citizens' lives, leading to a significant erosion of individual freedoms.

One of the most significant ways in which individual liberties are eroded under socialist regimes is through the suppression of free speech and dissent. Socialist states often seek to silence any opposition or criticism of the government, resulting in a lack of political freedoms. Citizens are not allowed to express their opinions freely or participate in meaningful political discourse, leading to a stifling of creativity and innovation.

Furthermore, socialist economies are known for their inefficiency and lack of innovation. The state's control over the means of production and distribution often leads to a lack of competition and incentive for innovation. As a result, resources are misallocated, and economic stagnation becomes the norm. This not only hinders economic development but also limits individuals' opportunities to improve their standard of living.

The unequal distribution of wealth and resources is another consequence of socialist policies. While the stated goal of socialism is to promote equality, the reality is that socialist regimes often concentrate power and wealth in the hands of a few. This leads to a small elite enjoying privileges and luxuries while the majority of the population struggles to make ends meet.

Moreover, socialist governments foster a dependency culture, where citizens become reliant on the state for their basic needs. This reliance on the state not only limits individual freedom but also hampers economic growth. The lack of incentives to work hard and innovate results in a stagnant economy and a decline in living standards.

In addition to the erosion of individual liberties, socialist systems are also plagued by corruption and a lack of accountability. The concentration of power in the hands of the state opens the door for corruption and abuse of power. This lack of transparency and accountability further undermines the trust between the government and its citizens.

Lastly, socialist industrial policies often lead to environmental degradation. The state's control over industries and lack of incentive for sustainable practices result in pollution, deforestation, and the destruction of natural resources. This not only harms the environment but also jeopardizes the well-being of future generations.

In conclusion, the erosion of individual liberties under socialist regimes is a significant concern. The suppression of free speech, the lack of innovation and economic stagnation, the unequal distribution of wealth, the dependency culture, the corruption, and lack of accountability, the environmental degradation, all contribute to the failure of socialism in promoting individual freedoms and improving living standards. It is crucial for educators and society at large to understand and address these issues to foster societies that prioritize and protect individual liberties.

The inefficiency and lack of innovation in socialist economies

In the realm of economic development, socialism has often been hailed as a means to achieve equality and social justice. However, a closer examination of socialist economies reveals a myriad of inefficiencies and a dearth of innovation that ultimately hinder progress and impede the betterment of society.

One of the fundamental shortcomings of socialist economies is their inability to efficiently allocate resources. Unlike in market-based capitalist systems, where the forces of supply and demand guide the distribution of goods and services, socialist economies rely on central planning. This centralized approach often results in bureaucratic red tape, long decision-making processes, and misallocation of resources. As a consequence, industries are burdened with inefficiencies, leading to lower productivity and slower economic growth.

Furthermore, the lack of innovation in socialist economies is a significant obstacle to progress. In capitalist societies, competition incentivizes companies to continually innovate and improve their products and services. However, in socialist economies, where the means of production are owned and controlled by the state, there is little motivation for innovation. The absence of market competition stifles creativity, as there is no reward for taking risks or pushing boundaries. Consequently, socialist economies lag behind their capitalist counterparts in terms of technological advancements and overall development.

Moreover, the unequal distribution of wealth and resources in socialist societies undermines the very principles of equality that socialism aims to achieve. While socialist rhetoric often emphasizes the elimination of social class distinctions, the reality is quite different. In practice, socialist regimes tend to concentrate power and wealth in the hands of a select few, leaving the majority of the population with limited access to resources and opportunities for advancement.

Additionally, the erosion of individual liberties under socialist regimes is a grave concern. Socialist governments often suppress free speech and dissent, stifling intellectual diversity and impeding the exchange of ideas. This lack of intellectual freedom hampers innovation and progress, as new ideas and perspectives are silenced and discouraged. Furthermore, the dependency culture fostered by socialist policies discourages individual initiative and self-reliance, ultimately hindering personal growth and societal advancement.

Moreover, the inability of socialist governments to provide adequate healthcare and education is a significant failing. Despite promises of universal access, socialist systems often struggle to deliver quality healthcare and education to their citizens. The lack of competition and innovation in these sectors results in subpar services, limited choices, and long waiting times. As a result, the quality of healthcare and education suffers, negatively impacting the overall well-being and future prospects of the population.

Furthermore, corruption and lack of accountability are pervasive in socialist systems. The concentration of power in the hands of the state creates fertile ground for corruption, as government officials wield significant control over economic resources and decision-making. This lack of transparency and accountability undermines the trust of the population and exacerbates the inefficiencies and inequalities already present in socialist economies.

Lastly, the environmental degradation resulting from socialist industrial policies cannot be ignored. In the pursuit of rapid industrialization, socialist regimes have often prioritized economic growth over environmental sustainability. As a result, socialist economies have been plagued by pollution, deforestation, and other forms of environmental degradation. The long-term consequences of these practices are detrimental to both human health and the planet's well-being.

In conclusion, despite its lofty promises of equality and social justice, socialism has consistently failed in economic development. The inefficiencies, lack of innovation, unequal distribution of wealth and resources, erosion of individual liberties, dependency culture, inadequate provision of healthcare and education, corruption, and environmental degradation all contribute to the unraveling of socialist economies. It is essential for educators and society at large to critically examine the shortcomings of socialism in order to pave the way for alternative economic systems that truly prioritize progress, innovation, and the well-being of all individuals.

The unequal distribution of wealth and resources in socialist societies

One of the most significant criticisms of socialist societies is the unequal distribution of wealth and resources. Although socialism promises equality and the eradication of poverty, the reality is often quite different. In fact, socialist economies tend to exacerbate wealth disparities, rather than alleviate them.

One key factor contributing to this inequality is the lack of incentive for individuals to work hard and excel in their professions. In socialist systems, the government controls production and distribution, meaning that individual effort is not rewarded proportionally. As a result, there is little motivation for individuals to strive for success, leading to a stagnant economy and limited wealth accumulation for the majority of the population.

Another contributing factor is the concentration of power in the hands of a select few. Socialist regimes often establish a ruling elite who control the allocation of resources and wealth. This concentration of power inevitably leads to corruption and favoritism, as those in authority exploit their positions for personal gain. The result is a small group of individuals who amass significant wealth while the majority of the population struggles to make ends meet.

Furthermore, socialist systems often lack the mechanisms to address the diverse needs and aspirations of their citizens. In these societies, resources are typically allocated based on the government's priorities rather than the demands of the people. As a result, certain regions or industries may receive preferential treatment, while others are neglected. This leads to regional disparities in wealth and resource distribution, further widening the gap between the rich and the poor.

Moreover, the absence of a market-based economy in socialist societies results in inefficiencies and a lack of innovation. Without competition, there is little incentive for businesses to improve their products or services. As a result, the economy stagnates, and the gap between the wealthy and the impoverished continues to widen.

In conclusion, the unequal distribution of wealth and resources is a fundamental flaw in socialist societies. Despite their purported goal of achieving equality and eradicating poverty, these systems often lead to increased disparities and concentrated wealth in the hands of a select few. The lack of incentives, concentration of power, and inefficiency of socialist economies all contribute to this unequal distribution. It is crucial for educators to understand these shortcomings and convey them to their students, as they play a vital role in shaping the future generation's understanding of economic systems and their implications.

The suppression of free speech and dissent in socialist states

One of the most alarming aspects of socialist states is the systematic suppression of free speech and dissent. Throughout history, we have witnessed numerous examples of how socialist regimes have curtailed the fundamental right to express one's opinions and ideas freely.

In these states, the ruling party maintains an iron grip on power, often monopolizing the media and controlling all forms of communication. Independent journalism is heavily censored or completely banned, and any criticism of the government is swiftly punished. This leads to a lack of transparency and accountability, allowing corruption and abuses of power to go unchecked.

Individuals who dare to speak out against the government face severe consequences. They are often subjected to harassment, intimidation, imprisonment, or even worse, as the state seeks to crush any form of dissent. The fear of reprisal forces citizens into silence, creating a climate of self-censorship and stifling any potential for intellectual growth and progress.

Furthermore, the suppression of free speech and dissent has a profound impact on the development of socialist economies. Without the ability to freely exchange ideas and challenge prevailing beliefs, innovation and creativity are stifled. Socialist states become stagnant and fail to keep pace with the rapidly changing global economy.

Additionally, the unequal distribution of wealth and resources in socialist societies exacerbates the suppression of free speech. The ruling elite, who control the levers of power, have a vested interest in maintaining the status quo. Any dissenting voices that question the unequal distribution of resources are swiftly silenced, as they pose a threat to the ruling party's grip on power.

The erosion of individual liberties under socialist regimes also extends to the erosion of basic human rights. Socialist governments often fail to provide adequate healthcare and education, leaving their citizens vulnerable and dependent on the state for their most basic needs. This dependency culture perpetuates the cycle of suppression, as individuals are afraid to speak out for fear of losing the limited support they receive from the government.

In conclusion, the suppression of free speech and dissent in socialist states is a grave concern that educators must address. By shedding light on the detrimental effects of this suppression, we can work towards creating a society that values and protects the fundamental right to free expression. Only through open dialogue and the free exchange of ideas can we foster innovation, accountability, and ultimately, improve the lives of citizens in socialist states.

The dependency culture fostered by socialist policies

One of the most detrimental effects of socialist policies is the creation of a dependency culture within societies. Under socialist regimes, the government assumes a central role in providing for its citizens, offering various social welfare programs and redistributing wealth. While this may initially seem like a noble endeavor, it ultimately leads to a culture of dependency and reliance on the state.

Socialist policies discourage individual initiative and self-reliance, as they promote the idea that the government is responsible for meeting the basic needs of its citizens. Instead of encouraging individuals to take responsibility for their own lives and strive for success, socialism fosters a mentality of entitlement, where individuals expect the government to provide for them from cradle to grave.

This dependency culture is detrimental to the overall progress and development of a society. When individuals become reliant on the state for their livelihoods, they lose the motivation to work hard and innovate. As a result, socialist economies often suffer from a lack of productivity and innovation, leading to economic stagnation.

Moreover, the dependency culture perpetuated by socialist policies erodes individual liberties. When the state holds the power to provide for its citizens, it also gains the authority to dictate how resources are allocated and how individuals should live their lives. This leads to a suppression of personal freedoms and a disregard for individual choices and preferences.

Another consequence of a dependency culture is the unequal distribution of wealth and resources. While socialist policies claim to promote equality, they often result in a small elite group controlling and distributing resources. This exacerbates social inequality and undermines the principles of fairness and equal opportunity.

Furthermore, socialist regimes tend to suppress free speech and dissent in order to maintain their control over the population. Criticism of the government or its policies is often met with censorship, imprisonment, or even violence. This stifles innovation and prevents the exchange of ideas necessary for societal progress.

Additionally, the inability of socialist governments to provide adequate healthcare and education is a direct result of the dependency culture they foster. When the government assumes responsibility for these essential services, it often leads to inefficiency, lack of accountability, and corruption. As a result, healthcare and education systems in socialist countries often lag behind, failing to meet the needs of the population.

Lastly, the dependency culture fostered by socialist policies also contributes to environmental degradation. Socialist industrial policies often prioritize production over environmental sustainability, leading to pollution, deforestation, and resource depletion. This not only harms the natural environment but also undermines the long-term sustainability of the economy.

In conclusion, the dependency culture fostered by socialist policies has far-reaching consequences. It discourages individual initiative, erodes personal freedoms, perpetuates inequality, stifles innovation, and hinders the provision of essential services. It is imperative for educators and society as a whole to understand these issues in order to avoid the failures and pitfalls of socialism and promote sustainable and equitable development.

The inability of socialist governments to provide adequate healthcare and education

One of the most glaring failures of socialist governments is their inability to provide adequate healthcare and education to their citizens. Despite their promises of equality and social justice, socialist regimes have repeatedly proven unable to deliver on these basic needs.

In socialist systems, healthcare and education are often centralized and controlled by the state. While this may seem like an efficient way to ensure equal access for all, the reality is far from ideal. Centralization leads to a lack of competition and innovation, resulting in a stagnant and inefficient system that fails to meet the diverse needs of the population.

Moreover, socialist governments often struggle with resource allocation. Limited funding and mismanagement frequently lead to a lack of proper infrastructure, medical supplies, and qualified personnel. The result is overcrowded hospitals, long waiting times, and a decline in the quality of care. Patients are forced to endure subpar conditions and inadequate treatment, ultimately leading to a decline in overall health outcomes.

Similarly, socialist governments' education systems suffer from similar deficiencies. While the rhetoric may emphasize equal access to education, the reality is that quality education becomes a privilege enjoyed by the few rather than a right for all. Underfunded schools, outdated materials, and underqualified teachers are common features of socialist education systems.

Moreover, the lack of competition and innovation stifles creativity and critical thinking, leaving students ill-prepared for the challenges of the modern world. Socialist regimes prioritize indoctrination rather than fostering a well-rounded education. Dissent and differing opinions are suppressed, and individuals are discouraged from questioning the status quo.

The result of these failures is a society that remains trapped in a cycle of poverty and stagnation. Without access to quality healthcare and education, individuals are unable to reach their full potential and contribute meaningfully to their economy and society.

In conclusion, the inability of socialist governments to provide adequate healthcare and education is a clear demonstration of the failure of socialism in economic development. The centralized control and lack of competition result in stagnant and inefficient systems that fail to meet the needs of the population. The erosion of individual liberties, the unequal distribution of resources, and the suppression of dissent further compound these failures. For educators, it is essential to understand these shortcomings and advocate for alternative systems that prioritize individual freedoms, innovation, and a market-based approach to healthcare and education. Only then can we truly provide our students with the tools they need to succeed and thrive in a rapidly changing world.

The corruption and lack of accountability in socialist systems

One of the most pervasive criticisms of socialist systems is the rampant corruption and lack of accountability that often plagues these societies. While socialism promises equality and fairness, the reality is often far from it. This subchapter will explore the various ways in which corruption thrives in socialist systems and the consequences it has on economic development and individual liberties.

Corruption is an inherent problem in any system, but it seems to be particularly prevalent in socialist economies. The concentration of power in the hands of a few government officials creates an environment ripe for abuse. Without the checks and balances of a free market system, individuals in positions of authority can easily exploit their power for personal gain.

One of the key reasons behind this corruption is the lack of accountability in socialist systems. Without a competitive market and the threat of losing customers or investors, there is little incentive for government officials to act in the best interest of the people. Instead, they focus on enriching themselves and their cronies, leading to a culture of bribery, embezzlement, and nepotism.

The consequences of this corruption are far-reaching. Firstly, it hinders economic development by diverting resources away from productive sectors and towards the pockets of corrupt officials. This misallocation of resources leads to economic stagnation and a lack of innovation, as funds that could be invested in research and development or infrastructure projects are siphoned off.

Moreover, corruption in socialist systems also erodes individual liberties. Dissent and free speech are suppressed, as those who speak out against the corrupt regime are often silenced or punished. This stifles creativity, innovation, and intellectual discourse, further exacerbating the economic stagnation.

The unequal distribution of wealth and resources is another consequence of corruption in socialist societies. While socialism promises equality, the reality is that corrupt officials amass vast fortunes while the majority of the population struggles to make ends meet. This exacerbates social divisions and fosters a sense of resentment and injustice among the people.

Lastly, the lack of accountability in socialist systems also affects the provision of basic necessities such as healthcare and education. Without proper oversight, funds meant for public services are often embezzled or mismanaged, leaving the most vulnerable members of society without access to these crucial services.

In conclusion, the corruption and lack of accountability in socialist systems have far-reaching consequences. Economic stagnation, erosion of individual liberties, unequal distribution of wealth, and inadequate provision of basic necessities are just some of the many issues that arise from this systemic problem. It is essential for educators to understand these challenges and educate others about the failure of socialism in economic development. Only through awareness and critical thinking can we hope to unravel the myths surrounding socialism and work towards more sustainable and accountable systems.

The environmental degradation resulting from socialist industrial policies

One of the many consequences of socialist industrial policies is the severe environmental degradation that occurs in these societies. While proponents of socialism often argue that this economic system is more focused on social equality and welfare, the reality is that it often leads to significant harm to the environment.

One of the main reasons for this is the lack of accountability and regulation in socialist economies. Without a free market and competition, there is little incentive for businesses to invest in environmentally friendly practices. In addition, the centralized planning characteristic of socialist economies often leads to inefficient allocation of resources, resulting in excessive pollution and waste.

Moreover, socialist regimes have historically prioritized rapid industrialization over environmental concerns. The drive to achieve self-sufficiency and economic growth often leads to the exploitation of natural resources without proper consideration for sustainability. Forests are clear-cut, rivers are polluted, and ecosystems are destroyed, all in the pursuit of industrial development.

Furthermore, the lack of individual liberties under socialist regimes hampers the ability of citizens to advocate for environmental protection. Free speech and dissent are suppressed, making it difficult for environmental activists to raise awareness and push for change. This lack of public participation in decision-making processes further exacerbates environmental problems.

Additionally, the inefficiency and lack of innovation in socialist economies hinder the development and implementation of clean technologies. Without the incentives provided by a market economy, there is little motivation for businesses to invest in research and development of environmentally friendly alternatives.

The unequal distribution of wealth and resources in socialist societies also plays a role in environmental degradation. The concentration of power and wealth in the hands of the state or ruling elite often leads to the exploitation of natural resources for their own benefit, while neglecting the needs and rights of the general population.

In conclusion, the environmental degradation resulting from socialist industrial policies is a significant issue that cannot be ignored. The lack of accountability, inefficiency, and centralized planning characteristic of socialist economies, coupled with the prioritization of rapid industrialization over environmental concerns, all contribute to the harm inflicted on the environment. It is essential for educators and society as a whole to understand and acknowledge the negative environmental consequences of socialism, in order to foster a more sustainable and responsible approach to economic development.

The failure of socialist states to provide basic necessities and improve living standards

In this subchapter, we will delve into the inherent flaws of socialist states that have led to their failure in providing basic necessities and improving living standards for their citizens. Despite the promises of equality and prosperity, socialist economies have consistently fallen short in meeting the basic needs of their populations.

One of the fundamental problems with socialist systems is their centralized planning and control of resources. Instead of allowing the market to allocate resources efficiently, socialist governments attempt to dictate production and distribution. This top-down approach leads to inefficiencies, shortages, and the inability to meet the demands of the population. Basic necessities such as food, housing, and clothing become scarce, leaving citizens to struggle to meet their daily needs.

Moreover, the lack of innovation and competition in socialist economies further exacerbates the problem. Without the incentives provided by the free market, there is little drive for entrepreneurs and businesses to innovate and improve productivity. This results in stagnant economic growth and an inability to create new job opportunities and increase living standards.

In addition to economic stagnation, socialist regimes often erode individual liberties in their pursuit of equality. The suppression of free speech and dissent stifles creativity and prevents the exchange of ideas necessary for progress. Citizens are unable to voice their concerns and hold the government accountable, leading to a lack of transparency and widespread corruption.

Furthermore, socialist systems tend to foster a dependency culture, where citizens rely heavily on the government for their basic needs. This creates a sense of entitlement and hampers individual initiative and self-reliance. Instead of empowering individuals to improve their own lives, socialist policies perpetuate a cycle of dependence and inhibit social mobility.

The failure of socialist governments to provide adequate healthcare and education is another critical aspect. Despite promising universal access to these essential services, socialist states often struggle to meet the demand due to limited resources and inefficiencies. As a result, healthcare and education systems suffer from inadequate funding, outdated infrastructure, and a lack of quality.

Lastly, the environmental degradation resulting from socialist industrial policies cannot be ignored. In their pursuit of rapid industrialization, socialist states often prioritize economic growth over environmental concerns. This leads to pollution, deforestation, and the depletion of natural resources, further compromising the living standards of the population.

In conclusion, the failure of socialist states to provide basic necessities and improve living standards can be attributed to the inefficiency, lack of innovation, erosion of individual liberties, unequal distribution of wealth, and corruption inherent in socialist systems. Educators must be aware of these shortcomings to provide a comprehensive understanding of the consequences of socialist policies and promote alternative approaches to economic development.

Chapter 2: The Economic Stagnation Caused by Socialism

The central planning fallacy in socialist economies

The central planning fallacy in socialist economies is a critical aspect that has contributed to the failure of socialism in economic development. This subchapter aims to unravel the myths surrounding this fallacy and shed light on its detrimental effects on various aspects of society.

In socialist economies, the government assumes the role of central planner, attempting to control and coordinate all economic activities. This approach stems from the belief that central planning can allocate resources efficiently and ensure equitable distribution of wealth. However, history has shown that this belief is flawed.

One of the most evident consequences of central planning is economic stagnation. When the government controls production, investment, and pricing decisions, it hampers market forces that drive innovation, competition, and efficiency. As a result, socialist economies often suffer from a lack of progress and fail to keep up with the rapid advancements seen in capitalist systems.

Moreover, the erosion of individual liberties is a crucial concern under socialist regimes. The concentration of power in the hands of the government leads to the suppression of free speech and dissent. Socialist states often prioritize the interests of the ruling elite over the rights and aspirations of their citizens, leading to a stifling of creativity and individual expression.

Another significant consequence of central planning is the unequal distribution of wealth and resources. While socialism claims to promote equality, the reality is quite different. Central planners tend to favor certain groups or individuals, leading to a concentration of wealth and power in the hands of a few. This further exacerbates social and economic disparities within society.

Additionally, socialist policies foster a dependency culture, discouraging individual initiative and self-reliance. When the state provides for the basic needs of its citizens, there is little incentive for individuals to strive for personal growth and productivity. This dependency hinders economic progress and perpetuates a cycle of stagnation.

Furthermore, socialist governments often struggle to provide adequate healthcare and education. The central planning approach fails to account for the diverse needs and preferences of individuals. Consequently, healthcare systems are often plagued by inefficiency, long waiting times, and limited access to quality care. Similarly, education systems suffer from a lack of innovation and fail to prepare individuals for the rapidly evolving job market.

Lastly, the central planning fallacy exposes socialist systems to corruption and a lack of accountability. When the government has unchecked control over economic decisions, there is a higher likelihood of bribery, favoritism, and misuse of public funds. This corruption further hampers economic development and undermines public trust in the system.

In conclusion, the central planning fallacy in socialist economies has had far-reaching consequences, contributing to their failure in economic development. It has resulted in economic stagnation, erosion of individual liberties, unequal distribution of wealth, suppression of free speech, fostered a dependency culture, inadequate healthcare and education, corruption, and environmental degradation. It is essential for educators and the wider public to understand these consequences to foster informed discussions about the flaws of socialism and the importance of alternative economic systems.

The misallocation of resources and capital in socialist systems

One of the fundamental flaws of socialist systems is the misallocation of resources and capital, which leads to economic inefficiency and stagnation. In these systems, the government controls and owns the means of production, deciding how resources should be allocated and what industries should receive capital investment. However, this centralized decision-making often results in the misallocation of resources, as the government lacks the necessary knowledge and incentives to make efficient choices.

In socialist economies, the lack of market mechanisms and price signals hampers the efficient allocation of resources. Without the price mechanism to guide decision-making, there is no accurate way to assess the relative scarcity and value of goods and services. As a result, resources are often directed towards politically favored sectors or industries, rather than being allocated based on consumer demand or the potential for profitability. This leads to a misallocation of resources, where industries that are inefficient or unproductive receive disproportionate amounts of capital, while more innovative and productive sectors are neglected.

Furthermore, the lack of competition and incentives for innovation in socialist economies exacerbates the problem of resource misallocation. Without the pressure to compete and innovate in order to survive in the market, firms in socialist systems have little motivation to improve productivity or efficiency. This lack of innovation further exacerbates the misallocation of resources, as outdated and inefficient production methods persist, hindering economic growth and development.

The misallocation of resources and capital in socialist systems also results in an unequal distribution of wealth and resources. As the government controls and allocates resources, it has the power to favor certain groups or individuals, leading to cronyism and corruption. This leads to a concentration of wealth and power in the hands of the political elite, while ordinary citizens are left with limited opportunities and access to resources.

Additionally, the misallocation of resources in socialist systems often leads to the failure of providing basic necessities and improving living standards. Limited resources are often wasted on grandiose projects or military expenditures, while essential services such as healthcare and education are underfunded and neglected. This results in inadequate healthcare systems, a lack of access to quality education, and a lower standard of living for the general population.

In conclusion, the misallocation of resources and capital in socialist systems is a major factor contributing to their economic failure. The lack of market mechanisms, competition, and incentives for innovation leads to inefficient resource allocation, an unequal distribution of wealth, and the failure to provide basic necessities and improve living standards. Educators need to understand these issues in order to provide a comprehensive understanding of the failures of socialism and its impact on economic development.

The lack of incentives for productivity and innovation in socialist economies

One of the fundamental flaws of socialist economies is the lack of incentives for productivity and innovation. In a system where the means of production are owned and controlled by the state, there is little room for individual initiative and entrepreneurial spirit. As a result, productivity and innovation suffer, leading to economic stagnation and a decline in living standards.

In socialist economies, there is no reward for hard work or innovation. The state owns and controls all industries, which means that there is no private ownership or profit motive to drive individuals and businesses to excel. Without the prospect of personal gain or the fear of failure, there is little motivation for individuals to work hard or take risks. This lack of incentives leads to a culture of mediocrity and complacency, stifling productivity and hindering economic growth.

Moreover, the absence of competition in socialist economies further contributes to the lack of innovation. Without the pressures of competition, there is little need for businesses to invest in research and development or improve their products and services. As a result, technological advancements are slow, and industries become stagnant. This lack of innovation not only hampers economic growth but also limits the ability of socialist economies to compete in the global marketplace.

Furthermore, the unequal distribution of wealth and resources in socialist societies exacerbates the lack of incentives for productivity and innovation. In these systems, the state controls the allocation of resources and wealth, leading to a concentration of power in the hands of a few. This concentration of power discourages individuals from taking risks or pursuing entrepreneurial ventures since any potential gains would be unfairly distributed. As a result, talented individuals often choose to leave socialist economies in search of opportunities where their efforts will be rewarded.

In conclusion, the lack of incentives for productivity and innovation is a significant drawback of socialist economies. Without the prospect of personal gain, competition, and a fair distribution of resources, individuals have little motivation to work hard or innovate. This lack of productivity and innovation leads to economic stagnation, the erosion of individual liberties, and a decline in living standards. It is crucial for educators to understand these shortcomings to provide a comprehensive understanding of the failure of socialism in economic development.

The role of government control and bureaucracy in hindering economic growth

In the quest for economic development, one cannot ignore the detrimental impact of government control and bureaucracy. This subchapter aims to shed light on how these factors have hindered economic growth in socialist societies.

Socialism, with its central tenet of government control over the means of production, has failed miserably in achieving sustained economic growth. The heavy hand of the state in regulating industries and markets has stifled entrepreneurship and innovation. Bureaucratic red tape, complex regulations, and excessive licensing requirements have deterred potential investors and hindered the establishment of new businesses. As a result, socialist economies have been plagued by sluggish growth and economic stagnation.

Another consequence of government control has been the erosion of individual liberties. Socialist regimes have been notorious for suppressing free speech and dissent, stifling creativity, and curbing intellectual freedom. This has created a culture of conformity, hindering the free exchange of ideas and inhibiting innovation. Without the freedom to challenge the status quo and explore new possibilities, socialist economies have struggled to adapt to changing global dynamics and technological advancements.

Moreover, the unequal distribution of wealth and resources in socialist societies has further hindered economic growth. Instead of promoting equality, socialism has often resulted in the concentration of wealth and power in the hands of a few. This has discouraged investment, hampered social mobility, and created a culture of dependency rather than self-reliance.

The inefficiency and lack of innovation in socialist economies can also be attributed to the absence of market forces. Without the price mechanism to allocate resources efficiently, socialist governments have been unable to respond to changing demand and allocate resources effectively. This has led to chronic shortages, poor quality products, and a lack of consumer choice.

Furthermore, the corruption and lack of accountability in socialist systems have undermined economic growth. Centralized control over resources and industries has provided fertile ground for corruption, nepotism, and cronyism. The misallocation of resources and the diversion of funds into private pockets have hindered investment, distorted markets, and perpetuated inefficiency.

Lastly, socialist governments have failed to provide basic necessities and improve living standards for their citizens. The focus on collective ownership and central planning has often come at the expense of adequate healthcare, education, and infrastructure. Socialist states have struggled to provide quality public services and have fallen behind in areas such as healthcare technology and education innovation.

In conclusion, the role of government control and bureaucracy in hindering economic growth cannot be underestimated. The failure of socialism in economic development is evident in the economic stagnation, erosion of individual liberties, lack of innovation, unequal distribution of wealth, suppression of free speech, dependency culture, inadequate healthcare and education, corruption, and environmental degradation that have plagued socialist societies. Educators and those interested in the failure of socialism must recognize these detrimental effects and advocate for alternative economic systems that promote individual freedom, innovation, and market-driven growth.

The impact of excessive regulation and state ownership on economic development

In the quest for economic development, many socialist regimes have resorted to excessive regulation and state ownership, believing that central planning and control are the keys to prosperity. However, history has shown that these policies have only led to economic stagnation, the erosion of individual liberties, the lack of innovation, unequal distribution of wealth, suppression of free speech, fostered dependency culture, inadequate healthcare and education, corruption, environmental degradation, and the failure to provide basic necessities and improve living standards.

Excessive regulation stifles economic growth and innovation. When the state controls every aspect of the economy, it limits the ability of individuals and businesses to make their own decisions, hindering entrepreneurship and stifling creativity. This lack of innovation leads to economic stagnation, as industries fail to adapt to changing market demands and technological advancements.

State ownership of industries also hampers economic development. When the government controls major sectors such as energy, transportation, and telecommunications, it often lacks the incentive and efficiency to operate these industries effectively. State-owned enterprises tend to be plagued by bureaucratic inefficiencies, mismanagement, and lack of accountability. This hinders their ability to provide quality goods and services, hindering overall economic growth.

Moreover, excessive regulation and state ownership result in an unequal distribution of wealth and resources. Socialist regimes often claim to promote equality, but in reality, they concentrate power and wealth in the hands of a few elites. This leads to a society where the gap between the rich and the poor widens, as the ruling class benefits from state-controlled resources and privileges, while the majority of citizens struggle to make ends meet.

Additionally, socialist regimes suppress free speech and dissent, limiting the exchange of ideas and stifling political and intellectual discourse. This leads to a lack of critical thinking and innovation, as alternative viewpoints are silenced, and intellectual curiosity is discouraged. The absence of open dialogue hinders progress and inhibits the development of a vibrant and dynamic society.

Furthermore, socialist policies foster a dependency culture, as the state provides cradle-to-grave welfare programs. While these programs may seem beneficial in the short term, they create a culture of entitlement and discourage personal responsibility and self-reliance. This dependency on the state stifles individual initiative and hinders economic development.

Finally, socialist regimes often fail to provide adequate healthcare and education. Despite promises of universal access, state-controlled systems are often plagued by inefficiency, lack of funding, and subpar services. Citizens are denied the opportunity to choose their healthcare providers or access quality education, resulting in a decline in overall standards of living.

In conclusion, excessive regulation and state ownership have a detrimental impact on economic development. The failure of socialism in economic development is evident in its contribution to economic stagnation, erosion of individual liberties, lack of innovation, unequal distribution of wealth, suppression of free speech, fostered dependency culture, inadequate healthcare and education, corruption, environmental degradation, and the failure to provide basic necessities and improve living standards. It is crucial for educators to understand these failures and teach the lessons of history, promoting policies that foster economic freedom, innovation, and individual liberties for the betterment of society as a whole.

Chapter 3: The Erosion of Individual Liberties under Socialist Regimes

The suppression of political dissent and freedom of speech

In the realm of socialist regimes, the suppression of political dissent and the erosion of freedom of speech have been pervasive, hampering the development and progress of societies. This subchapter aims to unravel the myths surrounding these issues by shedding light on the detrimental effects they have had on the economic, social, and political fabric of nations.

Socialist governments, driven by their desire to maintain control and perpetuate their ideology, have consistently stifled any form of political opposition. Dissenting voices, whether from intellectuals, activists, or ordinary citizens, have been silenced through a range of repressive measures. These include censorship, surveillance, imprisonment, and even violence. By suppressing political dissent, these regimes have denied their citizens the right to freely express their opinions and participate in the democratic process.

The consequences of this suppression have been far-reaching. By eliminating the space for open dialogue and debate, socialist states have hindered the development of innovative ideas and policies. Without the constructive criticism and diverse perspectives that dissent brings, these societies have stagnated economically and failed to adapt to changing global dynamics. The lack of competition and alternative viewpoints has led to inefficiencies and a lack of innovation in socialist economies.

Furthermore, the unequal distribution of wealth and resources in socialist societies has exacerbated social tensions. The lack of freedom of speech and political dissent has allowed those in power to consolidate their wealth and suppress any attempts at redistribution. This has perpetuated a dependency culture, where citizens are reliant on the state for basic necessities, leading to a cycle of poverty and limited upward mobility.

Moreover, the suppression of free speech has also hindered the provision of adequate healthcare and education. Without an open exchange of ideas, socialist governments have been unable to access the expertise and knowledge necessary to improve these essential services. Consequently, citizens have been deprived of quality healthcare and education, further exacerbating the societal inequalities perpetuated by socialist regimes.

Corruption and lack of accountability have also plagued socialist systems, as the absence of dissenting voices allows those in power to act with impunity. This has resulted in widespread environmental degradation, as socialist industrial policies prioritize short-term gains over long-term sustainability. Additionally, the failure of socialist states to provide basic necessities and improve living standards can be attributed to the lack of accountability and transparency within these systems.

In conclusion, the suppression of political dissent and freedom of speech under socialist regimes has had detrimental effects on economic development, individual liberties, societal well-being, and environmental sustainability. Educators and those interested in understanding the failures of socialism must recognize the importance of free speech and dissent as catalysts for progress and the protection of human rights. Only by addressing these issues can we learn from the mistakes of the past and strive for a more inclusive and prosperous future.

The restriction of individual rights and personal freedoms in socialist societies

In the realm of socialism, the restriction of individual rights and personal freedoms has become a pervasive issue that cannot be ignored. While proponents of socialism argue that it promotes equality and social justice, the reality is far from the idealistic vision they paint. This subchapter will delve into the various ways in which individual liberties are curtailed and personal freedoms are stifled under socialist regimes.

One of the most glaring consequences of socialism is the erosion of individual liberties. Socialist governments often impose strict regulations and controls on the economy, which inevitably extend to the personal lives of citizens. The state's heavy-handed intervention often dictates what individuals can and cannot do, hindering their ability to make independent choices and pursue their own aspirations.

Furthermore, the inefficiency and lack of innovation in socialist economies further exacerbate the restriction of individual rights. Without the incentives provided by a free-market system, innovation and entrepreneurship are stifled. This lack of progress not only hampers economic development but also limits the opportunities available to individuals, restricting their ability to exercise their personal freedoms.

The unequal distribution of wealth and resources is another consequence of socialist societies. While proponents argue that socialism aims to eradicate poverty and promote equality, the reality is often quite different. Socialist governments tend to concentrate power and wealth in the hands of a few, leading to a stark divide between the elite ruling class and the rest of the population. This unequal distribution of resources further restricts the personal freedoms and opportunities available to the majority of citizens.

Moreover, the suppression of free speech and dissent is a common characteristic of socialist states. Socialist governments often view any form of opposition as a threat to their authority and resort to censorship, intimidation, and even violence to suppress opposing viewpoints. This suppression of free speech not only restricts individual rights but also stifles the exchange of ideas and innovation necessary for societal progress.

In addition, the dependency culture fostered by socialist policies further restricts individual freedoms. Socialist states often provide extensive social welfare programs, creating a culture of reliance on the government. This dependency limits citizens' ability to make independent choices and take charge of their own lives, trapping them in a cycle of reliance and restricting their personal freedoms.

Furthermore, socialist governments often fail to provide adequate healthcare and education, despite promising to do so. The centralized control and lack of competition in socialist systems result in inefficiencies and a lack of resources, ultimately compromising the quality and accessibility of essential services. This failure to meet basic needs further restricts individuals' rights and limits their ability to improve their living standards.

Lastly, the corruption and lack of accountability in socialist systems contribute to the restriction of individual rights. The concentration of power in the hands of a few enables corruption to thrive, as accountability mechanisms are weakened or nonexistent. This corruption not only undermines the trust between citizens and the state but also restricts individuals' ability to exercise their rights and seek justice.

In conclusion, the restriction of individual rights and personal freedoms in socialist societies is a troubling reality that cannot be overlooked. From the erosion of individual liberties to the suppression of dissent and the unequal distribution of wealth, socialist regimes consistently fail to uphold the rights and freedoms of their citizens. Educators must be aware of these issues to foster a critical understanding of socialism's failures and the consequences it has on economic development, personal liberties, and societal progress.

The use of propaganda and censorship to control the narrative in socialist states

In the realm of socialist states, the manipulation of information through propaganda and censorship has long been employed as a powerful tool to control the narrative and maintain a grip on power. This subchapter aims to shed light on this disturbing aspect of socialist regimes, exploring how it has contributed to the failure of socialism in economic development.

Propaganda, often disguised as state-controlled media, is a cornerstone of socialist governments' efforts to shape public opinion. By inundating citizens with a carefully crafted narrative, these regimes effectively stifle dissent and maintain a façade of popular support. Educators must understand the insidious nature of propaganda and teach their students to critically analyze information, distinguishing fact from fiction.

Censorship is another key mechanism employed by socialist states to suppress free speech and maintain control. By controlling access to information and limiting the flow of ideas, these regimes limit the potential for innovation, progress, and economic development. Educators play a crucial role in empowering their students to question authority, challenge censorship, and advocate for the freedom of expression.

The consequences of propaganda and censorship in socialist states are far-reaching. Economic stagnation is a direct result of stifled innovation and the suppression of dissenting voices. The unequal distribution of wealth and resources is perpetuated by a system that controls the narrative to maintain the status quo. The erosion of individual liberties, such as freedom of speech and assembly, leads to a society devoid of diversity of thought and stifles progress.

Furthermore, socialist policies often foster a dependency culture, as the state controls the provision of essential services like healthcare and education. This leaves citizens reliant on a system that fails to adequately meet their needs, resulting in subpar healthcare and education outcomes. Corruption and lack of accountability are rife in socialist systems, as the absence of a free press and independent judiciary allow those in power to act with impunity.

Lastly, the environmental degradation resulting from socialist industrial policies is often overlooked. The pursuit of rapid industrialization without regard for ecological consequences has led to severe environmental crises in socialist states. Educators must educate their students about the importance of sustainable development and the need for responsible economic policies.

In conclusion, the use of propaganda and censorship to control the narrative in socialist states has contributed to the failure of socialism in economic development. Educators have a vital role in exposing these tactics, empowering their students to think critically, and advocating for the protection of individual liberties, innovation, and accountability. By unraveling the myths surrounding socialism, educators can equip future generations with the knowledge necessary to avoid repeating the mistakes of the past.

The lack of independent judiciary and rule of law in socialist systems

One of the fundamental pillars of a democratic society is the presence of an independent judiciary and a strong rule of law. These components ensure that justice is served impartially, that citizens' rights are protected, and that the government is held accountable for its actions. However, in socialist systems, the lack of an independent judiciary and rule of law has been a consistent problem, leading to a multitude of issues and failures.

One of the most significant consequences of the absence of an independent judiciary in socialist systems is the erosion of individual liberties. Without the checks and balances provided by an impartial judiciary, the government gains unchecked power, often leading to the suppression of free speech and dissent. Citizens are unable to voice their opinions without fear of retribution, resulting in an environment of fear and oppression.

Moreover, the inefficiency and lack of innovation in socialist economies can be directly linked to the absence of an independent judiciary. When the government has complete control over the economy, there is no room for competition or the entrepreneurial spirit that drives innovation. This leads to economic stagnation and the inability to adapt to changing global markets.

Additionally, the unequal distribution of wealth and resources in socialist societies is exacerbated by the lack of an independent judiciary. Without proper oversight, those in power can manipulate the system to their advantage, leading to corruption and a concentration of wealth in the hands of a few. This further widens the gap between the rich and the poor, perpetuating social and economic disparities.

Furthermore, the dependency culture fostered by socialist policies is reinforced by the lack of accountability and transparency in the government. When the state provides for all the needs of its citizens, there is little incentive for individuals to take responsibility for their own lives. This leads to a culture of dependency, hindering personal growth and stifling individual initiative.

The absence of an independent judiciary also impacts the provision of basic necessities and the improvement of living standards. Without proper oversight, socialist governments often fail to effectively allocate resources, resulting in inadequate healthcare and education systems. The lack of accountability and corruption further exacerbate these problems, leaving citizens without access to quality services.

Lastly, the environmental degradation resulting from socialist industrial policies is a direct consequence of the absence of an independent judiciary. Without proper regulations and enforcement, industries can freely exploit natural resources, leading to irreversible damage to ecosystems and communities.

In conclusion, the lack of an independent judiciary and rule of law in socialist systems has far-reaching consequences. It leads to the erosion of individual liberties, economic stagnation, unequal distribution of wealth, suppression of free speech, dependency culture, inadequate healthcare and education, corruption, and environmental degradation. These failures highlight the inherent flaws of socialism in promoting sustainable economic development and ensuring the well-being of its citizens.

Chapter 4: The Inefficiency and Lack of Innovation in Socialist Economies

The absence of market mechanisms and price signals in socialist economies

One of the fundamental flaws of socialist economies is the absence of market mechanisms and price signals. Unlike market-based economies, where prices are determined by the forces of supply and demand, socialist economies rely on central planning and government control. This absence of market mechanisms leads to a host of problems and inefficiencies that have been widely observed in socialist countries around the world.

Without market mechanisms, there is no efficient allocation of resources. In a market-based economy, prices serve as signals for producers and consumers, guiding them to make rational decisions about what to produce and consume. However, in a socialist economy, prices are often set arbitrarily by the government, leading to misallocation of resources. This results in chronic shortages of essential goods and services, as well as surpluses of items that are not in demand.

Furthermore, the absence of market mechanisms stifles innovation and inhibits economic growth. In a market-based economy, competition and the profit motive drive innovation and technological advancements. However, in a socialist economy, where the means of production are owned and controlled by the state, there is little incentive for individuals and businesses to innovate. As a result, socialist economies tend to lag behind market-based economies in terms of technological progress and economic growth.

The lack of market mechanisms also leads to an unequal distribution of wealth and resources. In a market-based economy, individuals are rewarded based on their productivity and contribution to society. However, in a socialist economy, wealth and resources are often distributed based on political favoritism and central planning. This leads to a small elite controlling the majority of the wealth, while the rest of the population struggles to make ends meet.

Moreover, the absence of market mechanisms in socialist economies often results in the erosion of individual liberties and the suppression of free speech and dissent. Without the ability to freely exchange goods and ideas in the marketplace, individuals are subject to government control and censorship. Socialist regimes have a history of stifling political dissent and suppressing basic freedoms, as seen in countries like the former Soviet Union and North Korea.

In addition to these problems, socialist economies often foster a dependency culture, as government-provided healthcare and education are often inadequate. The lack of competition and market incentives in these sectors leads to a decline in quality and innovation, leaving citizens reliant on the state for essential services.

Furthermore, socialist systems are plagued by corruption and a lack of accountability. The concentration of power in the hands of the state creates opportunities for corruption and abuse of authority, leading to the misallocation of resources and the enrichment of a few at the expense of the many.

Finally, socialist industrial policies often result in environmental degradation. The absence of market mechanisms leads to a lack of incentives for businesses to adopt environmentally friendly practices. As a result, socialist countries have a history of industrial pollution and environmental degradation.

In conclusion, the absence of market mechanisms and price signals in socialist economies leads to a host of problems, including economic stagnation, the erosion of individual liberties, the lack of innovation, the unequal distribution of wealth, the suppression of free speech, the fostering of a dependency culture, the inability to provide adequate healthcare and education, corruption and lack of accountability, and environmental degradation. These issues have been observed in socialist countries throughout history, highlighting the failure of socialism in economic development.

The lack of competition and incentives for efficiency in socialist systems

In the realm of economic development, one of the most significant challenges faced by socialist systems is the lack of competition and incentives for efficiency. While proponents of socialism argue that it promotes equality and social justice, the reality is that it often leads to economic stagnation, inefficiency, and a lack of innovation.

One of the fundamental flaws of socialist systems is the absence of competition. In a free-market capitalist system, competition drives businesses to constantly improve their products and services in order to attract consumers. In contrast, socialist economies often lack this essential driving force, as the state controls most, if not all, industries. Without competition, there is no pressure for businesses to innovate, invest in research and development, or streamline their operations to become more efficient.

Furthermore, the lack of competition in socialist systems also results in a dearth of incentives for efficiency. In capitalist economies, businesses strive to be efficient in order to maximize profits and gain a competitive edge. However, in socialist systems, there is little motivation for enterprises to be efficient, as there are no profits to be made and no competition to outperform. As a result, resources are often misallocated, production processes are inefficient, and overall economic growth is hindered.

Another consequence of the lack of competition and incentives for efficiency in socialist systems is the unequal distribution of wealth and resources. Without the market forces of supply and demand, socialist governments are tasked with the responsibility of distributing resources. However, this centralized approach often leads to favoritism, corruption, and an unequal distribution of wealth. While the intention may be to promote equality, the reality is that socialist systems often result in a small elite class benefiting at the expense of the majority.

Moreover, the suppression of free speech and dissent in socialist states further exacerbates the lack of innovation and efficiency. In order for societies to progress, there must be room for critical thinking, open dialogue, and the exchange of ideas. However, socialist regimes tend to stifle dissenting voices and control the flow of information, stifling creativity, and hindering progress.

In conclusion, the lack of competition and incentives for efficiency in socialist systems has dire consequences for economic development. The absence of competition leads to economic stagnation, inefficiency, and a lack of innovation. Furthermore, it results in an unequal distribution of wealth and resources, the suppression of free speech and dissent, and the overall degradation of living standards. It is essential for educators to understand and teach these realities in order to provide a comprehensive understanding of the failure of socialism in economic development.

The stifling effect of state control on entrepreneurship and innovation

In the grand scheme of economic development, one cannot overlook the detrimental impact of state control on entrepreneurship and innovation. This subchapter aims to unravel the myths surrounding socialism's failure in this regard, shedding light on the various ways in which state control hampers the growth and progress of societies.

Entrepreneurs are the backbone of any thriving economy. They are the risk-takers, the visionaries, and the drivers of innovation. However, under socialist regimes, the heavy hand of state control creates a hostile environment for these individuals to flourish. The economic stagnation caused by socialism is a direct result of this stifling effect. With excessive regulations, bureaucratic red tape, and limited opportunities for private enterprise, innovation is suffocated, and economic growth becomes stagnant.

Moreover, the erosion of individual liberties under socialist regimes further exacerbates the problem. Entrepreneurship requires freedom - freedom to create, freedom to compete, and freedom to succeed. By curbing these fundamental rights, socialism robs individuals of the motivation and incentives necessary for entrepreneurial ventures to thrive. In the absence of a free market, where supply and demand dictate economic decisions, innovation becomes a rarity, and progress slows to a crawl.

Another consequence of state control is the inefficiency and lack of innovation in socialist economies. Central planning and top-down decision-making strip away the agility and adaptability that are essential for thriving economies. Innovation requires experimentation, trial and error, and the ability to respond swiftly to changing market conditions. These elements are stifled under a system where the state holds a monopoly on economic decision-making.

Furthermore, the unequal distribution of wealth and resources in socialist societies exacerbates the problem. Rather than fostering an environment where wealth creation benefits all members of society, socialism concentrates power and resources in the hands of a few. This lack of equitable distribution stifles entrepreneurship and innovation by leaving the majority without the means to invest in their ideas and create new ventures.

The suppression of free speech and dissent in socialist states also plays a significant role in hampering entrepreneurship and innovation. Critical thinking, creativity, and diverse perspectives are essential drivers of innovation. However, in socialist societies, the fear of retribution and the lack of free speech discourage individuals from voicing their ideas and challenging the status quo.

In conclusion, the stifling effect of state control on entrepreneurship and innovation is a central theme in unraveling the myths surrounding socialism's failure in economic development. The heavy hand of state control, erosion of individual liberties, lack of innovation, unequal distribution of wealth, suppression of free speech, and dependency culture all contribute to the downfall of socialist economies. To truly foster economic growth and progress, societies must embrace the principles of free markets, individual freedoms, and limited government intervention. Only then can entrepreneurship and innovation thrive, leading to sustainable development and improved living standards for all.

Chapter 5: The Unequal Distribution of Wealth and Resources in Socialist Societies

The concentration of power and wealth in the hands of the ruling elite

The concentration of power and wealth in the hands of the ruling elite has been a pervasive problem in socialist societies throughout history. Despite claims of equality and social justice, the reality is that socialism often leads to a small group of individuals amassing immense power and wealth, while the majority of the population struggles to make ends meet.

One of the main reasons for this concentration of power is the lack of economic freedom and competition that is inherent in socialist economies. Without the incentive to innovate and create wealth, the ruling elite is able to maintain their control over the means of production and accumulate wealth at the expense of the rest of society.

Furthermore, the erosion of individual liberties under socialist regimes contributes to the concentration of power. Socialist governments often suppress free speech and dissent, making it difficult for individuals to challenge the ruling elite and advocate for their own rights and interests. This lack of accountability leads to corruption and further entrenches the power of the ruling elite.

In addition to the concentration of power, socialist societies also suffer from an unequal distribution of wealth and resources. While the ruling elite enjoy a lavish lifestyle, the majority of the population struggles to access basic necessities and improve their living standards. This inequality is exacerbated by the dependency culture fostered by socialist policies, which discourage individual initiative and self-reliance.

The inefficiency and lack of innovation in socialist economies also contribute to the concentration of power and wealth. Without the market forces of supply and demand to guide resource allocation, socialist governments often misallocate resources and fail to meet the needs of the population. This leads to economic stagnation and further entrenches the power of the ruling elite.

Moreover, socialist governments often fail to provide adequate healthcare and education for their citizens. Despite promises of universal access to these basic necessities, the reality is that socialist states struggle to provide quality services to their populations. This further exacerbates the inequality and concentration of power in these societies.

Lastly, the environmental degradation resulting from socialist industrial policies cannot be overlooked. The lack of incentives for environmental conservation and the disregard for the long-term consequences of industrial activities lead to severe environmental damage. This not only affects the well-being of the population but also further concentrates power and wealth in the hands of the ruling elite, who are often the beneficiaries of these destructive industrial practices.

In conclusion, the concentration of power and wealth in the hands of the ruling elite is a grave concern in socialist societies. The failure of socialism to deliver on its promises of equality and social justice has led to economic stagnation, the erosion of individual liberties, the unequal distribution of wealth, the suppression of free speech, the fostered dependency culture, the inability to provide basic necessities, the corruption and lack of accountability, the environmental degradation, and the failure to improve living standards. Educators must recognize these failures in order to promote a more effective and equitable approach to economic development.

The lack of upward mobility and social mobility in socialist societies

One of the fundamental promises made by socialist ideologies is the notion of equal opportunity for all individuals to succeed and move up the social ladder. However, a closer examination of socialist societies throughout history reveals a stark contrast to this idealistic vision. This subchapter aims to shed light on the lack of upward mobility and social mobility that plagues socialist societies, providing educators with valuable insights to understand the failure of socialism in economic development.

In many socialist regimes, the economic stagnation caused by centralized planning and government control severely hampers opportunities for individuals to improve their economic standing. The lack of market competition and incentives for innovation result in stagnant economies that fail to create new jobs or foster entrepreneurship. As a result, individuals often find themselves trapped in low-paying, unfulfilling jobs with little to no prospects for advancement.

Furthermore, the erosion of individual liberties under socialist regimes further exacerbates the lack of upward mobility. Socialist governments tend to suppress free speech and dissent, stifling the ability of individuals to voice their concerns and advocate for change. This leads to a culture of conformity and discourages individuals from challenging the status quo, limiting their ability to improve their social and economic standing.

Moreover, the unequal distribution of wealth and resources in socialist societies further widens the gap between the privileged few and the masses. Rather than providing equal opportunities for all, socialist regimes often concentrate power and wealth in the hands of a select few elites, creating a rigid class system that inhibits social mobility. This unequal distribution of resources prevents individuals from accessing quality education, healthcare, and basic necessities, further hindering their ability to improve their living standards.

Additionally, the dependency culture fostered by socialist policies perpetuates the lack of upward mobility. By providing extensive social welfare programs and safety nets, socialist governments inadvertently discourage individuals from striving for success. The assurance of basic necessities without the need for hard work or initiative fosters a culture of dependency, stifling individuals' motivation to improve their economic standing.

In conclusion, the lack of upward mobility and social mobility in socialist societies is a significant failure of these systems. Educators must be aware of these shortcomings to provide a comprehensive understanding of the consequences of socialism. By unraveling the myths surrounding socialism's ability to provide equal opportunities, educators can equip future generations with knowledge and critical thinking skills necessary to navigate the complexities of economic development.

The impact of income redistribution on economic growth and prosperity

Income redistribution, a key tenet of socialist ideologies, has long been touted as a means to achieve economic growth and prosperity for all members of society. However, history has shown that this approach has failed to deliver on its promises, often resulting in negative consequences for the economy and its citizens.

One of the most significant impacts of income redistribution is the economic stagnation it causes. By taking from the productive members of society and redistributing their wealth to others, incentives for hard work, innovation, and entrepreneurship are diminished. This leads to a decline in overall economic productivity and growth, hindering the potential for prosperity.

Moreover, the erosion of individual liberties is another consequence of income redistribution under socialist regimes. As the state gains more control over the distribution of wealth, individual freedom and economic autonomy are curtailed. This stifles creativity, inhibits risk-taking, and discourages the pursuit of personal goals, thereby impeding economic progress.

Additionally, the inefficiency and lack of innovation in socialist economies have been widely documented. Centralized planning, a hallmark of socialist systems, often results in bureaucratic red tape, inefficiencies, and a lack of market responsiveness. This hampers economic growth and stifles technological advancements, leaving societies behind their capitalist counterparts.

Income redistribution also leads to the unequal distribution of wealth and resources in socialist societies. While it may aim to achieve a more equitable distribution, in reality, it often creates a new elite class that benefits disproportionately from the redistribution efforts, exacerbating social and economic disparities rather than alleviating them.

Furthermore, the suppression of free speech and dissent is a common feature of socialist states. Governments that control the distribution of resources often silence opposition and suppress alternative viewpoints, hindering innovation, and hindering progress. This lack of intellectual diversity further contributes to economic stagnation and hampers the free exchange of ideas necessary for growth.

The dependency culture fostered by socialist policies is also detrimental to economic growth and prosperity. By providing extensive welfare programs and handouts, individuals become reliant on government support rather than striving for self-sufficiency and personal development. This perpetuates a cycle of dependency, hindering economic progress and stifling individual potential.

Moreover, socialist governments often fail to provide adequate healthcare and education despite promises of universal access.

Centralized control over these essential services often leads to inefficiencies, shortages, and a decline in quality, leaving citizens without access to the necessary tools for personal and economic development.

The corruption and lack of accountability in socialist systems further hinder economic growth and prosperity. When the state controls the distribution of wealth, it creates opportunities for corruption, bribery, and favoritism. These practices divert resources away from productive uses and undermine the foundations of a healthy economy.

Lastly, the environmental degradation resulting from socialist industrial policies cannot be overlooked. The lack of market incentives for environmental conservation and the disregard for private property rights often lead to the overexploitation of natural resources, pollution, and ecological damage. This not only harms the environment but also hampers long-term sustainable economic growth.

In conclusion, income redistribution, a key pillar of socialism, has had a detrimental impact on economic growth and prosperity. The failure of socialist states to deliver on their promises, the economic stagnation caused by income redistribution, the erosion of individual liberties, the inefficiency and lack of innovation, the unequal distribution of wealth, the suppression of free speech, the dependency culture, inadequate healthcare and education, corruption and lack of accountability, environmental degradation, and the failure to provide basic necessities and improve living standards all highlight the negative consequences of income redistribution in socialist societies. It is essential for educators and society at large to understand these impacts and consider alternative approaches that foster individual freedom, free markets, and entrepreneurship for sustainable economic growth and prosperity.

Chapter 6: The Suppression of Free Speech and Dissent in Socialist States

The use of propaganda and state-controlled media to manipulate public opinion

In the realm of socialism and economic development, one cannot ignore the pivotal role played by propaganda and state-controlled media in shaping public opinion. Throughout history, socialist regimes have adeptly exploited these tools to further their political agendas, suppress dissent, and maintain a stranglehold on power. This subchapter aims to unravel the myths surrounding the use of propaganda and state-controlled media, shedding light on its detrimental effects on societies and individuals.

Propaganda, as a means of communication, is employed to influence public perception, manipulate emotions, and control the narrative. Socialist governments have mastered the art of harnessing this powerful tool to perpetuate their ideologies and maintain a stranglehold on power. By carefully crafting messages, disseminating distorted information, and suppressing alternative viewpoints, these regimes create a skewed reality that favors their own interests while undermining the truth.

State-controlled media acts as a mouthpiece for socialist governments, serving as a propaganda machine that disseminates biased information, suppresses dissent, and promotes the ruling party's agenda. Journalists and media outlets are forced to toe the party line, stifling independent thought and critical analysis. This erosion of journalistic integrity further perpetuates the manipulation of public opinion, hindering any meaningful debate or critique of the government's policies.

The consequences of such manipulation are far-reaching and devastating. The unequal distribution of wealth and resources in socialist societies is often concealed through propaganda, presenting a false image of equality and social justice. The erosion of individual liberties under socialist regimes is downplayed, as state-controlled media portrays these measures as necessary for the greater good. The inefficiency and lack of innovation in socialist economies are masked by propagandistic claims of progress and success.

Moreover, the suppression of free speech and dissent in socialist states is justified through propaganda that labels opposition as counterrevolutionary or anti-socialist. This fosters a culture of fear and conformity, stifling any genuine expression of ideas or criticism. The dependency culture fostered by socialist policies is perpetuated through propaganda that promotes the idea of reliance on the state, discouraging self-reliance and personal initiative.

Furthermore, the inability of socialist governments to provide adequate healthcare and education is often obscured through propaganda that highlights select success stories while suppressing the systemic failures. The corruption and lack of accountability in socialist systems are conveniently swept under the rug, protecting the ruling elite from scrutiny. The environmental degradation resulting from socialist industrial policies is downplayed or outright denied through propaganda that portrays the government as a steward of nature.

Ultimately, the use of propaganda and state-controlled media to manipulate public opinion serves as a powerful tool for socialist regimes to maintain their grip on power and perpetuate their failed economic systems. Educators play a crucial role in unveiling these manipulative narratives, equipping students with the critical thinking skills necessary to discern truth from propaganda. By exposing the myths surrounding the use of propaganda and state-controlled media, educators can empower future generations to question authority, challenge prevailing narratives, and strive for a more just and prosperous society.

The persecution of political opponents and dissidents in socialist regimes

One of the most disturbing aspects of socialist regimes is the relentless persecution of political opponents and dissidents. This subchapter aims to shed light on the grave consequences that individuals face when they dare to challenge the ruling party's ideology or question its policies.

In socialist regimes, the fear of dissent runs deep. The ruling party, driven by its insatiable hunger for power, employs a range of tactics to suppress any opposition. These tactics include arbitrary arrests, forced disappearances, torture, and even executions. Political opponents are often labeled as enemies of the state and are subjected to public shamings and character assassinations.

The erosion of individual liberties under socialist regimes is a direct consequence of the ruling party's desire to maintain control. Freedom of speech, assembly, and association are severely curtailed, leaving citizens with no recourse to express their grievances or organize for change. In these societies, the government becomes the ultimate arbiter of truth, and any dissenting voice is swiftly silenced.

Furthermore, the inefficiency and lack of innovation in socialist economies exacerbate the persecution of political opponents. When the government controls all means of production and stifles competition, there is no incentive for progress or improvement. Innovation is stifled, and economic stagnation becomes the norm. In such an environment, the ruling party becomes increasingly paranoid, viewing any challenge to its authority as a threat to its survival.

The unequal distribution of wealth and resources in socialist societies also plays a significant role in the persecution of political opponents. Those who are seen as a threat to the ruling party's power are often deprived of basic necessities such as food, housing, and healthcare. This creates a culture of dependency, where individuals are coerced into silence for fear of losing what little they have.

Moreover, the corruption and lack of accountability in socialist systems enable the ruling party to act with impunity. The leaders and their cronies amass vast wealth and exploit their positions for personal gain, while the rest of the population suffers. Dissidents who attempt to expose this corruption are met with harsh reprisals, further solidifying the ruling party's grip on power.

In conclusion, the persecution of political opponents and dissidents in socialist regimes is a dark reality that cannot be ignored. Educators must be aware of these grave injustices and teach their students about the dangers of unchecked power and the erosion of individual liberties. By understanding the failure of socialism in protecting basic rights and fostering economic development, we can work towards building societies that prioritize freedom, equality, and justice for all.

The restriction of freedom of assembly and association in socialist societies

One of the most glaring failures of socialist societies is the severe restriction of freedom of assembly and association. In these regimes, the government tightly controls the ability of citizens to gather and form groups, stifling any form of dissent and undermining the very essence of democracy.

Under socialist rule, the state views any kind of assembly or association as a potential threat to its authority. As a result, strict laws and regulations are put in place to suppress the formation of independent organizations and to ensure that any gatherings are closely monitored and controlled. This not only curtails the right to peaceful assembly but also hampers the development of civil society and the ability of citizens to come together to address common concerns and advocate for change.

In socialist societies, the government often justifies these restrictions by claiming that they are necessary for maintaining social order and preventing counter-revolutionary activities. However, in reality, these restrictions are used to suppress political opposition, stifle dissent, and maintain the grip of the ruling party on power.

The erosion of freedom of assembly and association is just one example of how individual liberties are systematically undermined under socialist regimes. Alongside the suppression of free speech and dissent, the restriction on assembly effectively silences any voices that challenge the government's policies or demand accountability.

Furthermore, the lack of freedom of assembly and association hampers innovation and economic development. In a free society, associations and gatherings foster collaboration and the exchange of ideas, leading to new discoveries and advancements. However, under socialism, these opportunities for innovation are severely limited, stifling economic growth and progress.

Moreover, the restriction of freedom of assembly and association exacerbates the already unequal distribution of wealth and resources in socialist societies. Without the ability to form independent organizations or advocate for their rights collectively, marginalized groups are effectively silenced and unable to challenge the status quo.

In conclusion, the restriction of freedom of assembly and association is a significant problem in socialist societies. It not only undermines individual liberties but also hampers economic development, perpetuates inequality, and stifles progress. Educators and those interested in the failures of socialism must recognize the importance of these issues and work towards promoting the value of freedom of assembly and association in any society. Only by doing so can we ensure a more just, prosperous, and democratic future.

Chapter 7: The Dependency Culture Fostered by Socialist Policies

The creation of a welfare state and entitlement mentality in socialist systems

One of the key features of socialist systems is the establishment of a welfare state, which aims to provide a safety net for all citizens. However, while this may sound like a noble idea in theory, the reality is that it often leads to the development of an entitlement mentality among the population. This subchapter will explore how the creation of a welfare state in socialist systems has contributed to the failure of socialism in economic development.

In socialist systems, the government is responsible for providing a range of social benefits, including healthcare, education, and housing. While these services may initially be seen as essential to improving living standards, they also create a sense of dependency among the population. Citizens come to expect the government to take care of their every need, rather than taking personal responsibility for their own well-being.

This entitlement mentality has several detrimental effects. Firstly, it leads to a lack of innovation and productivity. When individuals rely on the government for their basic needs, they have little incentive to work hard and be entrepreneurial. As a result, socialist economies tend to be stagnant and fail to keep up with the rapid pace of global economic development.

Furthermore, the unequal distribution of wealth and resources in socialist societies is exacerbated by the welfare state. While the government may claim to provide for all citizens equally, the reality is that those with political connections or who are part of the ruling elite often receive preferential treatment. This leads to a concentration of wealth and power in the hands of a few, while the majority of the population remains impoverished.

Another consequence of the entitlement mentality in socialist systems is the erosion of individual liberties. As the government becomes increasingly involved in the lives of its citizens, it often imposes strict regulations and controls to ensure compliance. Free speech and dissent are suppressed, as any criticism of the government is seen as a threat to the socialist ideology.

Moreover, the inefficiency and corruption that are inherent in socialist systems become even more pronounced with the establishment of a welfare state. Bureaucratic red tape and lack of accountability make it difficult for the government to effectively provide adequate healthcare and education to its citizens. This results in a decline in the quality of these services, further perpetuating the cycle of dependency.

Lastly, the environmental degradation resulting from socialist industrial policies cannot be ignored. In an effort to achieve rapid industrialization, socialist regimes often prioritize economic growth over environmental sustainability. This leads to the destruction of natural resources and pollution, which not only harms the environment but also negatively impacts the health and well-being of the population.

In conclusion, the creation of a welfare state and entitlement mentality in socialist systems has contributed to the failure of socialism in economic development. The dependency culture fostered by socialist policies, the unequal distribution of wealth and resources, the erosion of individual liberties, the inefficiency and lack of innovation, the suppression of free speech and dissent, the inability to provide adequate healthcare and education, the corruption and lack of accountability, the environmental degradation, and the failure to provide basic necessities and improve living standards all highlight the detrimental effects of the welfare state in socialist systems. It is crucial for educators and those interested in understanding the failure of socialism to recognize the role of the welfare state in perpetuating these issues and consider alternative approaches to economic development.

The disincentives for work and productivity in socialist societies

The disincentives for work and productivity in socialist societies are a fundamental aspect that has contributed to the failure of socialism in economic development. This subchapter aims to shed light on the various factors that have hindered progress and stifled individual initiative in these societies.

One of the primary reasons for the economic stagnation caused by socialism is the lack of motivation to work and be productive. In socialist systems, there is often a lack of reward for hard work and innovation. Since wealth and resources are distributed equally, there is little incentive for individuals to strive for excellence or take risks. This results in a culture where mediocrity is rewarded and ambition is discouraged.

Furthermore, the erosion of individual liberties under socialist regimes has had a detrimental impact on work and productivity. In order to maintain control, socialist governments often impose strict regulations and suppress freedoms. This stifles creativity and innovation, as individuals are afraid to express dissenting opinions or challenge the status quo. Without the freedom to think and act independently, individuals are less likely to contribute to the growth and development of their societies.

The inefficiency and lack of innovation in socialist economies also play a significant role in discouraging work and productivity. Centralized planning and state control of key industries lead to bureaucratic red tape and a lack of flexibility. This hampers entrepreneurship and stifles competition, resulting in a lack of innovation and technological advancement. Without the drive for efficiency and the ability to adapt to changing market conditions, socialist economies lag behind their capitalist counterparts.

Moreover, the unequal distribution of wealth and resources in socialist societies creates a sense of hopelessness and discourages hard work. When individuals see that their efforts will not lead to personal gain or improvement in their living standards, they become demotivated. This creates a dependency culture, where individuals rely on the state for basic necessities rather than striving for self-sufficiency and progress.

In addition, the suppression of free speech and dissent in socialist states further exacerbates the disincentives for work and productivity. When individuals are not allowed to express their opinions or criticize government policies, they are less likely to contribute constructively to societal development. This lack of open dialogue and exchange of ideas stifles creativity and innovation, hindering progress.

Overall, the disincentives for work and productivity in socialist societies have played a significant role in their failure to provide adequate healthcare, education, and improve living standards. The lack of motivation, erosion of individual liberties, inefficiency, unequal distribution of wealth, suppression of free speech, and dependency culture are all factors that have hindered progress and contributed to economic stagnation. It is crucial for educators to understand these challenges in order to provide a comprehensive analysis of the failures of socialism and promote alternative economic systems that foster innovation, individual liberties, and productivity.

The impact of dependency on government assistance on individual initiative and self-reliance

In today's society, there is an increasing trend towards dependency on government assistance. This subchapter aims to explore the consequences of this dependency on individual initiative and self-reliance. By understanding the negative impact of relying on government assistance, educators can equip their students with the knowledge and skills to strive for personal success and avoid the pitfalls of dependency.

One of the key effects of government assistance is the erosion of individual initiative. When individuals become reliant on the government for their basic needs, such as food, housing, and healthcare, they may lose the motivation to work hard and pursue their own goals. This lack of initiative can lead to a decline in productivity, innovation, and economic growth. Educators play a vital role in instilling a sense of personal responsibility and ambition in their students, encouraging them to take control of their own lives and strive for success.

Furthermore, government assistance can foster a dependency culture, where individuals come to expect handouts rather than working to improve their own circumstances. This culture of dependency perpetuates inequality and hinders social mobility. Educators must emphasize the importance of self-reliance and encourage their students to seek opportunities for personal and professional growth, rather than relying on the government for support.

Another consequence of dependency on government assistance is the limited availability of resources for those truly in need. Socialist policies often result in an unequal distribution of wealth and resources, as the government tries to provide for everyone. This can lead to inefficiency and a lack of resources for those who genuinely require assistance. Educators should highlight the importance of personal responsibility and self-reliance, ensuring that students understand the potential consequences of relying solely on government support.

In conclusion, the impact of dependency on government assistance on individual initiative and self-reliance is multifaceted and far-reaching. It erodes personal ambition, fosters a culture of dependency, and limits resources for those truly in need. Educators have a crucial role to play in educating their students about the dangers of dependency and empowering them to take control of their own lives. By emphasizing personal responsibility, ambition, and self-reliance, educators can equip their students with the tools necessary to strive for personal success and contribute to the betterment of society.

Chapter 8: The Inability of Socialist Governments to Provide Adequate Healthcare and Education

The lack of quality and accessibility in healthcare systems under socialism

One of the key failures of socialism that often goes unnoticed or underestimated is the lack of quality and accessibility in healthcare systems. While socialist regimes often promise equal access to healthcare for all, the reality is often far from it.

In socialist economies, the government controls and owns the healthcare system, leading to inefficiency, lack of innovation, and unequal distribution of resources. The government's central planning and bureaucracy stifle competition and discourage private investment in healthcare. As a result, the quality of healthcare services deteriorates, and patients are often left without access to essential treatments and medications.

Moreover, the limited resources and lack of incentives in socialist economies create a dependency culture where individuals rely solely on the government for their healthcare needs. This further exacerbates the strain on the already burdened healthcare system, leading to long waiting times and inadequate care.

Furthermore, under socialist regimes, the erosion of individual liberties and suppression of free speech and dissent make it difficult for healthcare professionals to voice their concerns or criticize the government's policies. This lack of accountability and transparency leads to corruption and mismanagement of resources within the healthcare system.

The inability of socialist governments to provide adequate healthcare and education is not only a matter of quality but also accessibility. While healthcare is often touted as a universal right under socialism, the reality is that only the elite and well-connected receive the best medical care. The majority of the population is left with substandard facilities, long waiting times, and limited access to life-saving treatments.

Additionally, the environmental degradation resulting from socialist industrial policies further exacerbates the health issues faced by the population. The lack of regulation and accountability in socialist systems leads to the pollution of air, water, and land, causing significant health risks for individuals living in these areas.

In conclusion, the lack of quality and accessibility in healthcare systems is one of the many failures of socialism. The inefficiency, lack of innovation, unequal distribution of resources, and suppression of individual liberties all contribute to the inability of socialist governments to provide adequate healthcare for their citizens. It is crucial for educators to understand these shortcomings and educate others about the failures of socialism in improving living standards and providing basic necessities.

The limitations of government-run education systems in socialist societies

Education is a fundamental pillar of any society, shaping the future generation and providing them with the necessary skills and knowledge to succeed. However, in socialist societies, government-run education systems often fall short in meeting the needs of students and fail to foster an environment conducive to innovation and excellence.

One of the major limitations of government-run education systems in socialist societies is the lack of choice and competition. In these systems, the government maintains a monopoly over education, stifling any potential for alternative approaches or innovative ideas. This lack of competition leads to a stagnant and outdated curriculum, inhibiting the development of critical thinking and problem-solving skills among students.

Moreover, the unequal distribution of resources and wealth in socialist societies also affects the quality of education. The limited availability of resources and funding often leads to overcrowded classrooms, outdated teaching materials, and inadequate infrastructure. As a result, students from disadvantaged backgrounds are disproportionately affected, further perpetuating social inequality.

Furthermore, government-run education systems in socialist societies are often plagued by a lack of accountability and corruption. The centralized nature of these systems allows for little transparency and oversight, making it easier for officials to embezzle funds or engage in nepotism. This not only undermines the quality of education but also erodes public trust in the system.

In addition, the suppression of free speech and dissent in socialist states extends to the education sector. Critical thinking and open discussion are discouraged, as the government seeks to control the narrative and promote its ideology. This stifles creativity and intellectual growth among students, hindering their ability to think independently and contribute to society.

Furthermore, the focus on equality in socialist societies often results in a one-size-fits-all approach to education. Individual talents and interests are disregarded, and students are forced into a standardized curriculum that fails to cater to their unique abilities. This lack of personalization hinders the development of students' full potential and limits their future prospects.

In conclusion, government-run education systems in socialist societies suffer from numerous limitations that hinder the educational development of students. The lack of choice and competition, unequal distribution of resources, corruption, suppression of free speech, and the focus on equality over individual needs all contribute to the inefficiency and shortcomings of these systems. If socialist societies truly aim to provide adequate education and prepare their citizens for the challenges of the future, it is crucial to address these limitations and embrace reforms that prioritize innovation, accountability, and individual growth.

The impact of ideological indoctrination on educational institutions in socialist states

In the realm of education, socialist states have long been criticized for their heavy reliance on ideological indoctrination within educational institutions. This subchapter aims to shed light on the detrimental consequences of this practice, highlighting its negative impact on both students and society as a whole.

Socialist governments view education as a powerful tool for shaping the minds of future generations. Consequently, they have implemented policies that prioritize indoctrination over critical thinking and intellectual curiosity. By tightly controlling curricula, textbooks, and teaching materials, socialist states enforce a one-sided narrative that promotes their political agenda and suppresses alternative viewpoints.

The consequences of this ideological indoctrination are manifold. First and foremost, it stifles creativity and independent thought among students. Instead of fostering a spirit of innovation and critical analysis, educational institutions in socialist states become mere conduits for propagating state-sanctioned ideologies. This stifling of intellectual freedom leads to an erosion of individual liberties, one of the core criticisms of socialist regimes.

Moreover, the focus on ideological indoctrination comes at the expense of quality education. Rather than equipping students with the necessary skills and knowledge for personal and economic development, educational institutions in socialist states prioritize ideological conformity over academic excellence. As a result, the economic stagnation caused by socialism becomes further entrenched, as the next generation is ill-prepared to meet the challenges of a globalized and rapidly changing world.

Furthermore, the unequal distribution of wealth and resources in socialist societies is perpetuated through educational indoctrination. The curriculum often reinforces the idea of a class struggle, pitting the bourgeoisie against the proletariat. By promoting this narrative, socialist governments ensure that the masses remain dependent on the state, fostering a culture of dependency rather than individual initiative and entrepreneurship.

Another concerning consequence of ideological indoctrination is the suppression of free speech and dissent. Socialist states view alternative perspectives as threats to their power, leading to the censorship of ideas and the stifling of political opposition. This suppression hinders the development of a vibrant intellectual and political discourse, limiting the potential for innovation and progress.

As educators, it is crucial to recognize and challenge the impact of ideological indoctrination on educational institutions in socialist states. By promoting critical thinking, intellectual diversity, and an emphasis on academic excellence, educators can help break the cycle of indoctrination and empower students to become independent, innovative thinkers who can contribute to the betterment of society.

Chapter 9: The Corruption and Lack of Accountability in Socialist Systems

The concentration of power and lack of checks and balances in socialist governments

One of the most prominent criticisms of socialist governments is their tendency to concentrate power in the hands of a few individuals or a single ruling party. This lack of checks and balances can have detrimental effects on the overall functioning of the government and the well-being of its citizens.

In socialist systems, the ruling party often has complete control over the economy, media, and judiciary, leaving little room for dissent or opposition. This concentration of power stifles political pluralism and creates an environment where individual liberties are eroded. Educators have a crucial role in highlighting the importance of democratic principles and the need for a system of checks and balances to safeguard these liberties.

Moreover, the lack of competition and free-market mechanisms in socialist economies leads to economic stagnation and inefficiency. Without the incentive to innovate and the ability to respond to market demands, socialist economies struggle to keep up with the rapid advancements and technological progress seen in capitalist societies. Educators can shed light on the benefits of free-market competition and the role it plays in fostering economic growth and innovation.

In addition, the unequal distribution of wealth and resources is a prevalent issue in socialist societies. While the ideology of socialism aims to promote equality, the reality often falls short. The concentration of power allows those in control to manipulate resources and wealth, leading to a small elite benefiting at the expense of the majority.

Educators can help bring attention to the harmful consequences of this unequal distribution and the importance of a fair and just society.

Furthermore, the suppression of free speech and dissent in socialist states is a significant concern. Socialist governments often impose strict censorship and control over the media and public discourse, limiting the ability of individuals to express their opinions and hold their leaders accountable. Educators can emphasize the importance of freedom of speech and the role it plays in building a democratic society.

Overall, the concentration of power and lack of checks and balances in socialist governments can have wide-ranging negative impacts. Educators have a crucial role in educating individuals about these issues and fostering a critical understanding of the failures of socialism. By shedding light on the economic stagnation, erosion of individual liberties, inefficiency, unequal distribution of resources, suppression of free speech, and other issues associated with socialism, educators can contribute to a more informed and democratic society.

The prevalence of bribery, nepotism, and cronyism in socialist regimes

In the realm of political and economic systems, socialist regimes have often been associated with a high prevalence of bribery, nepotism, and cronyism. These vices have been significant contributors to the failure of socialism in economic development. Educators and those interested in understanding the failure of socialism need to recognize the detrimental impact of corruption in socialist societies.

Bribery, nepotism, and cronyism thrive in socialist regimes due to the lack of transparency, accountability, and checks and balances. In these systems, the state controls most economic activities, leaving little room for competition or fair market practices. As a result, individuals in positions of power often exploit their authority to extract personal gains, perpetuating a culture of corruption.

Nepotism, the favoring of family members in appointments or opportunities, is particularly rampant in socialist regimes. The lack of meritocracy and fair selection processes in these systems allows individuals in power to place their relatives in influential positions, regardless of their qualifications or capabilities. This nepotistic culture not only stifles innovation and progress but also creates a sense of disillusionment among the population, eroding their trust in the system.

Cronyism, the appointment of close associates or friends to key positions, is another common feature of socialist regimes. This practice leads to a concentration of power and resources in the hands of a select few, further exacerbating the unequal distribution of wealth and resources. Consequently, the majority of the population is left marginalized and deprived of opportunities, perpetuating a cycle of poverty and stagnation.

The prevalence of bribery, nepotism, and cronyism in socialist regimes also undermines individual liberties and suppresses free speech and dissent. Those who challenge the status quo or expose corruption are often silenced or face severe consequences. This lack of accountability and freedom of expression hinder the development of a thriving civil society and impede progress.

Moreover, the corruption and lack of accountability in socialist systems also extend to the provision of essential services such as healthcare and education. The misallocation of resources and embezzlement of funds intended for public welfare lead to inadequate and substandard services, leaving the population vulnerable and deprived of their basic needs.

In conclusion, corruption in the form of bribery, nepotism, and cronyism is pervasive in socialist regimes and has played a significant role in the failure of socialism in economic development. Educators and those interested in understanding the complexities and shortcomings of socialism must acknowledge the detrimental impact of corruption on individual liberties, economic progress, and the overall well-being of society. Only by recognizing and addressing these issues can we learn from the lessons of the past and strive for more effective and equitable systems of governance.

The absence of transparency and accountability mechanisms in socialist systems

One of the fundamental flaws in socialist systems is the absence of transparency and accountability mechanisms, which has detrimental effects on economic development and the overall well-being of its citizens. This subchapter aims to shed light on this critical issue and highlight the consequences of such a lack of transparency and accountability.

In socialist systems, the centralization of power and control often leads to a lack of transparency in decision-making processes. The government, being the sole authority, can make decisions without public scrutiny, which opens the door for corruption and favoritism. Without a transparent and accountable system, there is no way to hold those in power responsible for their actions, leading to a breeding ground for corruption and abuse of power.

Furthermore, the absence of accountability mechanisms in socialist systems stifles innovation and economic growth. In a free-market system, competition drives innovation, as companies strive to meet consumer demands and improve their products and services. However, in socialist economies, where the government controls most industries, there is little incentive for innovation. The lack of competition and accountability leads to inefficiencies and a stagnant economy.

Alongside the economic stagnation caused by socialism, the erosion of individual liberties is another consequence of the absence of transparency and accountability. Socialist regimes often suppress free speech and dissent, as they are seen as threats to the regime. Citizens are denied the right to express their opinions, leading to a stifling of creativity and intellectual growth.

The unequal distribution of wealth and resources is another consequence of the absence of transparency and accountability in socialist societies. Without an accountable system, the ruling elite can amass wealth and resources while neglecting the needs of the majority. This leads to a growing gap between the rich and the poor, exacerbating social inequalities.

Additionally, socialist policies foster a dependency culture, as the government takes on the role of providing healthcare and education. However, the inability of socialist governments to efficiently provide these basic necessities often leaves citizens reliant on an inefficient and inadequate system.

Lastly, the absence of transparency and accountability in socialist systems also contributes to environmental degradation. Socialist industrial policies often prioritize production over environmental concerns, leading to pollution and resource depletion. Without accountability, there is little incentive for the government to address these issues and protect the environment.

In conclusion, the absence of transparency and accountability mechanisms in socialist systems has far-reaching consequences. It results in economic stagnation, erosion of individual liberties, inequality, a dependency culture, and environmental degradation. Educators must be aware of these failures to provide a comprehensive understanding of the drawbacks of socialist systems and promote critical thinking among their students.

Chapter 10: The Environmental Degradation Resulting from Socialist Industrial Policies

The disregard for environmental conservation and sustainability in socialist economies

One of the many myths surrounding socialism is the notion that it is inherently beneficial for the environment. However, a closer examination of socialist economies reveals a disturbing trend of disregard for environmental conservation and sustainability. This subchapter aims to shed light on the environmental degradation resulting from socialist industrial policies and the failure of socialist states to prioritize the protection of natural resources.

In socialist economies, the pursuit of rapid industrialization often takes precedence over environmental concerns. The socialist governments, driven by the desire to compete with capitalist nations, prioritize the growth of heavy industries without adequately considering the environmental consequences. As a result, these economies witness high levels of pollution, deforestation, and depletion of natural resources.

Moreover, the lack of accountability and transparency in socialist systems exacerbates the problem. Without a free press or independent judiciary to hold the government accountable, environmental regulations are often ignored or poorly enforced. This leads to unchecked pollution and degradation of ecosystems, with no consequences for the responsible parties.

Additionally, the unequal distribution of wealth and resources in socialist societies further hampers environmental conservation efforts. The ruling elites, who control the means of production and resources, prioritize their own interests over the well-being of the environment.

This results in the exploitation of natural resources for personal gain, leading to irreversible damage to ecosystems and biodiversity.

Furthermore, the inefficiency and lack of innovation in socialist economies contribute to environmental degradation. Without the competitive pressures of a free market, there is little incentive for technological advancements that promote sustainable development. As a result, socialist economies lag behind in adopting environmentally friendly practices and technologies.

It is crucial for educators to understand the detrimental impact of socialist economic systems on the environment and to teach their students about the importance of environmental conservation. By debunking the myth that socialism inherently promotes sustainability, educators can equip their students with a more well-rounded understanding of the failures of socialism in economic development.

In conclusion, the disregard for environmental conservation and sustainability in socialist economies is a significant failure of socialism. The prioritization of rapid industrialization, the lack of accountability, the unequal distribution of resources, the inefficiency, and the lack of innovation all contribute to environmental degradation. Educators must address this failure and emphasize the importance of sustainable development to ensure a better future for generations to come.

The impact of state-controlled industries on pollution and resource depletion

One of the many detrimental effects of socialism on economic development lies in the impact of state-controlled industries on pollution and resource depletion. This subchapter aims to shed light on this critical issue, providing educators and readers interested in the failure of socialism with a comprehensive understanding of the environmental degradation resulting from socialist industrial policies.

Under socialism, the government assumes control over key industries, often leading to a lack of accountability and a disregard for environmental sustainability. State-controlled industries, driven by the pursuit of production quotas and centralized planning, tend to prioritize quantity over quality. As a result, environmental considerations, such as pollution control and resource conservation, are often overlooked or insufficiently addressed.

The consequences of this approach are severe. Socialist economies have a long history of being associated with high levels of pollution and resource depletion. Without the market mechanisms and incentives that promote responsible and sustainable practices in a free-market economy, state-controlled industries tend to be more wasteful and inefficient in their use of resources, leading to their rapid depletion.

Furthermore, the lack of competition and innovation in socialist economies hinders the development and adoption of cleaner and more sustainable technologies. In the absence of market forces that reward efficiency and innovation, state-controlled industries have little incentive to invest in environmentally friendly practices or to reduce their pollution levels.

The environmental degradation resulting from socialist industrial policies is not only harmful to the planet but also affects the well-being of the population. Pollution and resource depletion can lead to a decline in the quality of air, water, and soil, causing serious health issues for individuals living in affected areas.

By highlighting the link between state-controlled industries under socialism and their detrimental impact on the environment, this subchapter serves to further illustrate the broader theme of the failure of socialism. Educators and readers interested in the negative consequences of socialism, the erosion of individual liberties, and the inefficiency of socialist economies will find this subchapter particularly enlightening.

It provides a clear and evidence-based perspective on how socialist industrial policies contribute to environmental degradation, ultimately undermining the ability of socialist states to provide basic necessities and improve living standards for their citizens.

The failure of socialist governments to promote and enforce environmental regulations

In recent years, there has been an increasing concern about the impact of human activities on the environment. Governments around the world have taken various measures to address this issue and ensure the sustainable use of natural resources. However, it has become evident that socialist governments have been largely unsuccessful in promoting and enforcing environmental regulations. This subchapter aims to explore the reasons behind this failure and shed light on the consequences of neglecting environmental protection in socialist societies.

One of the main reasons for the failure of socialist governments to promote and enforce environmental regulations is their focus on economic development at the expense of environmental concerns. Socialist regimes often prioritize industrialization and rapid economic growth, neglecting the long-term consequences of their policies. This approach leads to the adoption of unsustainable practices, such as the excessive exploitation of natural resources and the disregard for pollution control measures.

Moreover, the inefficiency and lack of innovation in socialist economies contribute to the failure of environmental regulation. Socialist systems are characterized by central planning and state ownership of industries, which often results in bureaucratic inefficiencies and a lack of incentives for innovation. As a result, the development and implementation of effective environmental policies are hindered, and environmental degradation persists.

Furthermore, the unequal distribution of wealth and resources in socialist societies exacerbates the environmental degradation. The concentration of power and resources in the hands of a few elites leads to the exploitation of natural resources for personal gain, without considering the long-term consequences for the environment and the well-being of the population. The lack of accountability and transparency in socialist systems allows for corruption and the misuse of resources, further exacerbating environmental degradation.

The failure of socialist governments to provide basic necessities and improve living standards also contributes to environmental degradation. In many socialist states, the focus on economic development is often at the expense of providing adequate healthcare, education, and infrastructure. As a result, the population is forced to engage in activities that harm the environment, such as the unsustainable use of natural resources for subsistence purposes.

In conclusion, the failure of socialist governments to promote and enforce environmental regulations can be attributed to their focus on economic development, the inefficiency and lack of innovation in socialist economies, the unequal distribution of wealth and resources, and the failure to provide basic necessities and improve living standards. The consequences of neglecting environmental protection in socialist societies are evident in the environmental degradation and the long-term consequences for the well-being of the population. It is crucial for educators and policymakers to understand these issues and work towards finding sustainable solutions that balance economic development with environmental protection.

Chapter 11: The Failure of Socialist States to Provide Basic Necessities and Improve Living Standards

The inability of socialist systems to meet the basic needs of their populations

Introduction:

In recent years, there has been a surge in interest surrounding socialism and its potential as an alternative economic system. However, it is crucial to examine the historical failures of socialist systems in meeting the basic needs of their populations. This subchapter delves into the numerous challenges faced by socialist economies, ranging from economic stagnation and the erosion of individual liberties to the unequal distribution of wealth and resources. By exploring these issues, educators can gain a comprehensive understanding of the failure of socialism in economic development.

1. The economic stagnation caused by socialism:

Socialist economies have consistently struggled with economic stagnation, as central planning and state control hinder innovation and competition. The lack of market forces and profit incentives leads to inefficiencies, a lack of productivity, and ultimately, economic decline.

2. The erosion of individual liberties under socialist regimes:

Socialist regimes often prioritize the collective over individual rights, resulting in the suppression of free speech and dissent. This restriction on personal freedoms stifles creativity, innovation, and the ability to challenge the status quo, ultimately hindering economic progress.

3. The inefficiency and lack of innovation in socialist economies:

Socialist economies suffer from a lack of innovation due to the absence of competition and profit motives. Central planning fails to allocate resources efficiently, leading to the misallocation of capital and a lack of technological advancements.

4. The unequal distribution of wealth and resources in socialist societies:

Contrary to the promise of equality, socialist societies often face a significant wealth and resource disparity, with a small elite benefiting at the expense of the majority. The absence of market mechanisms and private property rights results in the concentration of power and resources in the hands of the ruling class.

5. The suppression of free speech and dissent in socialist states:

Socialist systems tend to silence dissenting voices and suppress free speech, inhibiting the exchange of ideas critical for societal progress. This lack of intellectual diversity stifles innovation and prevents the identification of potential flaws within the system.

Conclusion:

The inability of socialist systems to meet the basic needs of their populations is a result of economic stagnation, the erosion of individual liberties, inefficiency and lack of innovation, unequal distribution of wealth and resources, the suppression of free speech and dissent, and the dependency culture fostered by socialist policies. Educators must recognize these failures to provide a comprehensive understanding of the limitations and challenges associated with socialist economic models. By learning from these historical lessons, societies can strive towards more effective and equitable economic systems that truly meet the basic needs and improve the living standards of their populations.

The stagnation of living standards and lack of economic mobility in socialist societies

One of the key criticisms of socialist societies is the stagnation of living standards and the lack of economic mobility that accompanies them. Despite promising equality and prosperity for all, socialist regimes have consistently failed to deliver on these promises, leaving their citizens trapped in a state of economic and social immobility.

In socialist economies, the means of production are owned and controlled by the state, which leads to a lack of competition and innovation. Without the incentive of profit, individuals lack the motivation to work hard and strive for upward mobility. As a result, there is little room for personal development and the improvement of living standards.

Moreover, the unequal distribution of wealth and resources in socialist societies further exacerbates the stagnation of living standards. While socialist regimes often claim to prioritize equality, in reality, power and wealth tend to concentrate in the hands of a few party elites. This creates a stark divide between the ruling class and the ordinary citizens, with the latter left struggling to make ends meet.

Another consequence of socialism is the erosion of individual liberties. Socialist regimes suppress free speech and dissent, limiting the ability of individuals to voice their concerns and advocate for change. This lack of political freedom stifles innovation and prevents the development of new ideas that could drive economic growth and improve living standards.

Furthermore, socialist policies foster a dependency culture, where citizens rely on the state for their basic needs. Rather than encouraging self-sufficiency and personal responsibility, socialist governments provide inadequate healthcare and education, leaving their citizens reliant on the state for even the most basic necessities.

Corruption and lack of accountability are also prevalent in socialist systems. Without the checks and balances of a free market and democratic institutions, socialist governments are prone to abuse their power and prioritize personal gain over the well-being of their citizens. This further hampers economic development and perpetuates the stagnation of living standards.

Additionally, socialist industrial policies often lead to environmental degradation. Centralized planning and lack of market forces result in inefficient resource allocation and disregard for environmental sustainability. This not only harms the natural environment but also negatively impacts the health and well-being of the population.

In conclusion, the stagnation of living standards and lack of economic mobility in socialist societies are inherent flaws of the system. The erosion of individual liberties, the inefficiency and lack of innovation, the unequal distribution of wealth, and the suppression of free speech all contribute to the failure of socialism in providing adequate healthcare, education, and basic necessities. Furthermore, the corruption and lack of accountability, as well as the environmental degradation resulting from socialist industrial policies, further exacerbate the issues. It is crucial for educators to understand these failures in order to provide a comprehensive understanding of economic systems and promote informed decision-making among their students.

The contrast with market-based economies in terms of poverty reduction and quality of life improvements

In the realm of economic development, the failure of socialism becomes strikingly evident when comparing it with market-based economies in terms of poverty reduction and quality of life improvements. While socialism claims to prioritize equality and social welfare, it falls short in delivering on these promises, ultimately leading to economic stagnation, erosion of individual liberties, and an unequal distribution of wealth and resources.

One of the key areas where market-based economies excel is poverty reduction. By embracing free-market principles, these economies create an environment that fosters innovation, entrepreneurship, and job creation, resulting in higher incomes and better opportunities for individuals. In contrast, socialism's top-down approach stifles economic growth and discourages individual initiative, leading to persistent poverty and limited upward mobility. Educators must understand the detrimental impact of socialism on poverty reduction and advocate for market-based systems that empower individuals to improve their own economic situations.

Quality of life improvements, such as access to healthcare and education, are also severely hindered under socialism. Despite its promises to provide adequate healthcare and education for all, socialist governments consistently fail to deliver on these essential services. The inefficiency and lack of innovation inherent in socialist economies result in subpar healthcare systems and underfunded education programs. Educators must recognize the inability of socialist governments to provide these basic necessities and advocate for market-based approaches that promote competition and innovation, ultimately leading to better-quality services for all.

Moreover, socialism's suppression of free speech and dissent is a concerning aspect that directly impacts educators. In socialist states, the exchange of ideas and the pursuit of intellectual growth are often stifled, limiting the educational opportunities for both students and teachers. Educators must understand the importance of preserving freedom of speech and dissent as integral components of a thriving educational environment. Market-based economies, which prioritize individual liberties, provide a fertile ground for intellectual exchange and the generation of new ideas, ultimately benefiting educators and students alike.

In conclusion, the failure of socialism in economic development is evident when contrasting it with market-based economies in terms of poverty reduction and quality of life improvements. Educators must grasp the shortcomings of socialism, such as economic stagnation, erosion of individual liberties, and unequal distribution of wealth, and advocate for market-based approaches that foster innovation, empower individuals, and enhance the overall well-being of society. By doing so, educators contribute to a more informed and prosperous future for their students.

Conclusion: Lessons Learned and Implications for Economic Development

In this book, "Unraveling the Myths: The Failure of Socialism in Economic Development," we have examined the various aspects of socialism and its impact on economic development. From the failure of socialism to the erosion of individual liberties, the inefficiency and lack of innovation in socialist economies, the unequal distribution of wealth and resources, to the suppression of free speech and dissent, we have witnessed the detrimental consequences of socialist policies.

One of the key lessons learned from the failure of socialism is the importance of free markets and individual freedoms. Socialist regimes have consistently stifled economic growth and progress by implementing centralized control over industries and resources. The command economy model, which deprives individuals of their economic freedom, has proven to be inefficient and lacking in innovation. By contrast, free markets allow for competition, innovation, and entrepreneurship, leading to economic prosperity and development.

Socialism has also shown us the negative implications for the distribution of wealth and resources. While socialist societies claim to strive for equality, they often result in the concentration of power and wealth in the hands of a select few. This unequal distribution not only hinders economic development but also perpetuates social and economic disparities. In contrast, free-market economies provide opportunities for upward mobility and economic empowerment for all individuals.

Moreover, socialist regimes have consistently suppressed free speech and dissent, limiting the exchange of ideas and stifling intellectual progress. This has a detrimental effect on innovation and creativity, which are crucial for economic development. The importance of protecting individual liberties and fostering an environment that encourages open dialogue and diverse perspectives cannot be overstated.

Another important aspect to consider is the dependency culture fostered by socialist policies. By providing extensive social welfare programs, socialist governments create a reliance on the state, discouraging individual initiative and personal responsibility. This dependency hinders economic development and perpetuates a cycle of poverty.

Additionally, socialist systems have proven to be inadequate in providing essential services such as healthcare and education. The lack of competition and innovation in these sectors, coupled with government control, results in inefficiency and limited access to quality services. This further hampers economic development and negatively impacts the overall well-being of the population.

Furthermore, the lack of accountability and rampant corruption in socialist systems contribute to their failure. Without checks and balances, socialist governments often prioritize self-interest over the welfare of their citizens, leading to economic stagnation and the misallocation of resources.

Lastly, the environmental degradation resulting from socialist industrial policies cannot be ignored. The lack of incentives for sustainable practices and disregard for environmental regulations have led to severe ecological damage in socialist states.

In conclusion, the failure of socialism in economic development has taught us valuable lessons. The importance of free markets, individual liberties, accountability, and competition cannot be understated. It is crucial for educators and policymakers to understand the implications of socialism and advocate for economic systems that prioritize individual freedoms, innovation, and sustainable development. By learning from the mistakes of socialism, we can pave the way for a prosperous and equitable future.